3.

Peau

&

PRAISE FOR *Becoming A Humor Being*

"Steve Rizzo's book is an indispensable tool for maximizing your personal happiness. While challenging you to confront your inner fears and to explore the outside world, *Becoming A Humor Being* teaches you how to laugh at them both."

~ Anthony Robbins, Author
Awaken the Giant Within and *Unlimited Power*

"Laugh and the world laughs with you—Great advice for creating a joyful life."

~ Wayne Dyer, Author
Your Erroneous Zones and *Manifest Your Destiny*

"*Becoming A Humor Being* teaches how to draw on your sense of humor and higher self to help overcome life's bumps in the road. This book offers a wonderful set of tools to change your life and how you view it...forever."

~ John Gray, Author
Men Are from Mars, Women Are from Venus

"I receive more manuscripts to read than I want but out of guilt I dutifully read them before deciding to comment or not. If a book gets me to laugh and cry, it gets my highest rating. *Becoming A Humor Being* rates a 10. I laughed, cried and loved the truth and wisdom, which it contains. Only stories can reveal the truth and this book has all the stories you need to help you become a humor being in this lifetime.

~ Bernie Siegel, MD, Author
Love, Medicine & Miracles and *Prescriptions For Living*

"The longer I live the more I realize the impact of humor on life. I am convinced that life is 10 percent of what happens to me and 90 percent how I react to it. An 18th century Polish king said, "Good humor is the health of the soul, sadness its poison." So, here now, is a book that will help you to find humor everywhere and teach you how to apply it to every aspect of your life. As Dr. Seuss says, "From there to here, from here to there, funny things are everywhere!" I have been lucky enough to find it in the world of small children as my book and TV show proclaims, "Kids Say the Darndest Things." So does Steve Rizzo. So, let him re-introduce you to the Magic of Humor and thus help you to truly live life to its fullest.

~ Art Linkletter, Author
Kids Say the Darndest Things

"If you pick up this book you won't want to put it down. It made me want to become a better 'humor being.' "
~ Richard Carlson, Ph.D., Author
Don't Sweat the Small Stuff

"Through 'humor, hope, and love,' Steve Rizzo found his calling. He learned—and now teaches—how to be happy, to be free and to laugh out loud"
~ Marianne Williamson, Author
A Return to Love

Becoming A Humor Being

The Power to Choose a Better Way

STEVE RIZZO

FULL CIRCLE PUBLICATIONS
WADING RIVER, NEW YORK

Published by FULL CIRCLE PUBLISHING
440 Albany Avenue, Suite 6
Lindenhurst, New York 11757

Publisher's Cataloging-in-Publication Data
Rizzo, Steve.
    Becoming a humor being: the power to choose a better way /
    Steve Rizzo -- Lindenhurst, New York : Full Circle Pub., 2000.
        p.   cm.
    ISBN 0-9669895-0-3

    1. Wit and humor—psychological and spiritual aspects.   I. Title.
BF575.L3 R59   2000   98-89961
155.2'32   dc—21   CIP

PROJECT COORDINATION BY JENKINS GROUP, INC.

03 02 01 00 ⊛ 5 4 3 2

Printed in the United States of America

To my soul mate, Gina.
You are more than the wind beneath my wings.
You are the air that I breathe.

Contents

ॐ CONTENTS ॐ

$\mathcal{F}$oreword

Laughter is the best medicine—next to chicken soup.

In this warm and inspiring book, Steve Rizzo reveals how a sense of humor can empower each of us to overcome challenges in our personal and professional lives. He tells how laughter provides the strength and courage to overcome even seemingly insurmountable odds: chronic illness, disability, death, divorce, and unexpected job or career changes.

In *Becoming a Humor Being*, Steve takes us beyond the healing power of laughter. He discusses humor on a spiritual level, explaining that our *humor being* is a part of our higher self. Indeed, it is our *humor being* that gives us hope for a brighter and better tomorrow.

By telling his personal story, the author shares more than the gift of humor. He gives us a vehicle to love others and ourselves.

Through real-life anecdotes Steve reveals how humor frees us from anger, fear, and other negative feelings so that we can make loving and positive decisions—even under the most challenging of circumstances.

When we acknowledge our *humor beings* we can act more rationally, and achieve the success, happiness, and inner peace we desire.

Even negative beliefs that have been programmed since childhood can be overcome by listening to your *humor being*.

All of us have the choice of laughter.

Humor is not reserved for only a fortunate few. Steve Rizzo shows you how you can reprogram your way of thinking and allow the positive aspects of love and humor into your life.

Awaken your *humor being* and nurture your soul.

MARK VICTOR HANSEN
CO-AUTHOR *CHICKEN SOUP FOR THE SOUL*

Acknowledgments

I am truly grateful to many people who supported my work and helped make this book possible.

To my mother and father, whose gifts of unconditional love and humor are the foundation of this book.

To my wife, who is truly the motivation behind the motivator.

To my son, Sean, who always teaches me the importance of following your own path.

To my brother Michael, who is a living testament of what this book is all about.

To my brother Ricky, who shares a part of my past that no one else does.

To my sister, Laurie, whose inner strength keeps the family together.

A special thank you to Nancy Lauterbach, who believed in me from the beginning and helped launch my speaking career.

My thanks to Diane Driver, who took time out from her busy schedule to type out every single handwritten page of this book. (Believe me, with my handwriting that was not an easy task.)

I am indebted to Jeff Slutsky, whose knowledge and sick sense of humor helped me through the tough times. I am also indebted to Mark Hardy, who understands and shares my vision. To both Jeff and Mark, I value your friendship more than you will ever know.

⮫ Acknowledgments ⮪

To Nancy Vogl, who has a special way of performing miracles in my life.

To Michele Arden Stern, my valued personal assistant, for her continued dedication and energy. A very heartfelt thank you, thank you, thank you, thank you, thank you very much! (I think you get the point!)

To Maryanne Pepe, thank you for your artistic talents and humor insight.

To Mark Victor Hansen, Bernie Siegel, John Gray, Wayne Dyer, Art Linkletter, Richard Carlson, Anthony Robbins, and Marianne Williamson; thank you not only for the testimonials but also for your inspiration that has guided me on my journey.

And a special thank you to Ed and Marianne Primeau for their honesty, integrity and friendship.

I would like to thank everyone at the Jenkins Group for their professionalism, understanding, and sense of humor. A special thank you to Mary Jo, whose patience and expertise contributed to making this book a success.

To everyone at Five Star Speakers for their support and friendship.

And a very special thank you to Elizabeth Olin, who handles my calendar and busy schedule. I don't know how you do it, but without you I wouldn't have had time to write this book. Because of you I have peace of mind.

I want to thank all of the bureaus who book me and believe in my mission. I will be forever grateful to the National Speakers Association. You all have replenished my faith in people.

Finally, I would like to thank God for my dogs, Shelby, Casey, and Brandy—for they have shown me the true meaning of unconditional love.

And, thank you God for being my M.A.P.—my Manager, my Agent, and my Partner.

xii

Becoming A Humor Being

Introduction

Angels Don't Always Have Wings

"Take one step at a time," he said, "because the steps are the journey and with each step is an experience to encounter—a lesson to learn. You need them in order to truly embrace the fulfillment of the dream. To appreciate what you have is to appreciate how you earned it."

When I made the decision to give up my career as a stand-up comedian, I experienced many moments of doubt and sleepless nights. There were times when I questioned my sanity, but a greater force within kept pushing me. I had no idea where I was going. One thing was certain, I was on my way.

One night I woke up in a cold sweat. I looked at the

1

clock. It was 2:00 a.m. I could not get myself to stop shaking. Worse than that, I could not get my mind to stop thinking. Even though I had made a commitment to move forward with my new career, I still had doubts about what I was doing. My fears were getting the best of me and I felt I was losing all control. I guess the technical term for what I was experiencing was an anxiety attack.

I thought about waking my wife, but instead I decided to go into the living room and face this ordeal on my own. I sat on the couch and tried to stop my mind from racing. I kept asking myself what was wrong. My frustration turned to anger. I wanted to jump up and shout at the world. (If my wife had not been in the next room I would have done this.) I sat back down, put my face in a pillow and let the tears fall. This went on for some time. After a while my body was drained. I was totally exhausted, yet I felt a strange sense of inner peace.

My emotions had been building up for some time. I decided, right then and there, that I wanted answers. The only way I was going to get them was to be honest with myself, ask the right questions, and let it go.

The first words out of my mouth were, *"God give me patience! Oh, and I want it now!"* I smiled and felt relieved that I still had a sense of humor. (It truly is amazing how humor can aid us in our moments of pain.) I guess once a comedian, always a comedian. My conversation continued. *"I know doors have been opened, and I know I've come a long way. But I'm still confused. I need to know if I'm on the right path."*

I sat in silence and reflected upon the series of events that had led me to my current situation. I decided to put my thoughts in my journal. I proceeded to write out and then recite the following questions:

1. *Did I make the right decision to leave the world of stand-up comedy to become a speaker?*

2. *Do people need to hear what I have to say? Do they need to know how important humor can be in their lives? If so, how do I do it?*

3. *How can I help others, when I'm having a difficult time helping myself?*

These questions were my prayer. When I finished, I promised myself that I would be alert and in the right frame of consciousness to receive the answers. The next morning I woke up to a beautiful spring day and proceeded with my usual routine—thirty minutes of meditation, breakfast, and then to the health club. What happened next was a turning point in my life.

As I was leaving the health club, I noticed a man in the parking lot polishing a brand new red convertible Corvette. He was short in stature, with long brown uncombed hair, untrimmed beard, dark thick sunglasses and a tie-dye T-shirt. This guy looked like he should have been polishing a 1967 Volkswagen van with flowers and peace signs all over it.

I don't care for sports cars, especially Corvettes, but there was something about the contrast of this guy behind the wheel of that car that made me laugh. Trying not to show my amusement, I walked over and said, *"Nice car."*

"Thanks," he said. *"But they're tough to keep clean."* He moved over to the front end of the car to buff the headlight covers. It was then that I noticed the license plate read COMEDY with a handicap sign next to it. Now he really had my attention.

"Are you a comedian?" I asked.

"No."

"Why do you have comedy on your license plate?" I pursued.

"Because I always wanted to be a comedian," he explained. *"People need to laugh, especially today. I think our sense of humor is one of the greatest gifts God ever gave us. I would like to be a giver of this gift."*

I proceeded to tell him that I was a comedian, but he interrupted me and said, *"Excuse me, I'm not finished yet."* He continued, *"People need to know that they're OK. Humor can help them through hard times. But I guess that's the problem, most people don't even know they have this gift, let alone how to use it. And anyone who has the power to make people laugh or feel good in anyway is truly blessed."*

I just stood there, watching this guy who looked like a refugee from the 1960s buffing his car. He stopped, put down his rag, looked straight at me and said, *"You're a comedian aren't you?"*

"Yes," I replied.

"I saw you on TV," he said. *"Steve Rizzo, right?"*

I nodded. *"You're very funny,"* he said. *"Do you want to know why I have the handicap sign on my license plate?"*

"Yes. Why?"

"I hurt my back. Do you want to know how?"

I hesitated. *"How?"* I asked.

He said, *"From carrying too much weight. Instead of carrying a little at a time, I tried to carry the whole load at once. You are bound to hurt yourself when you do that."* He picked up his rag and continued to buff his car.

I was about to ask him what he was trying to carry when he interrupted me again. *"People do that a lot, you know? They set goals, have dreams and instead of enjoying the process, they expect immediate results, instant gratification and a guarantee that they're doing the right thing.*

"And when things don't go their way or as fast as they want, they panic and leave themselves open for fear and negativity to set in." He paused, shook his head and said, *"That type of thinking is bound to weigh them down. It's too much of a load for anyone to carry, because in reality there aren't any shortcuts. There are no guarantees—only choices, choices and faith."*

I didn't say a word. I just listened and watched as he shined his car. Then he stopped, looked at me and said, *"Do you want to know what one of the keys for fulfilling a dream is?"*

I didn't say anything, but to myself I thought, *"Oh God, here we go again!"*

"Take one step at a time," he said, *"because the steps are the journey, and with each step is an experience to encounter—a lesson to learn. You need them in order to truly embrace the fulfillment of the dream. To appreciate what you have is to appreciate how you earned it."* He laughed and said, *"Hey that's heavy. Maybe I should be a philosopher."*

He put the rag down and walked up to me. I couldn't see his eyes through his dark sunglasses, but I knew he was looking directly into mine. I said, *"Someday I will fulfill my dream. But until then I'm going to appreciate the step I'm on. I want to enjoy myself as I get there, not when I get there."*

He smiled and said, *"It was wonderful talking with you."* He reached out both of his hands, firmly held mine, and said, *"God bless you. You have a wonderful gift. Use it. Use it and share it with the world."*

The few people with whom I have shared this story believe this mysterious man was an angel from God. It's not my purpose, however, to prove the existence of angels or angelic happenings. The point is that someone I had never met before answered three direct questions to my prayers precisely the next day. This proves there is something greater about our existence than we think.

What is an angel, but a messenger from God? What is the difference if my mysterious friend was a being with supernatural divine powers or someone like you and me—someone who gave me the faith and hope I needed to move on with my life? Either way, it's divine intervention. He was a messenger from God. My prayers were answered.

Following the encounter with my mysterious friend, a massive flow of information kept coming my way. Situations and incredible opportunities confirmed I was on the right path. And that path became my mission.

Since I was committed to move forward, I was open to the universe and its unlimited abundance and to receive and take advantage of the serendipitous events that filled my life.

Throughout my travels, events led me to people who had overcome major tragedies in their lives, from financial disaster to the loss of a loved one. Some were physically or mentally challenged while others were diagnosed with cancer or infected with the HIV virus. In all cases, these people proclaimed that their sense of humor played a major role in either a full recovery or a total acceptance of their situation so that they could embrace the changes and lead productive lives in spite of their situations.

In part, humor was the answer to their prayers. To

some, it was their foundation. It enabled them to build pillars of hope and faith. Ironically, their stories paved the way towards my own healing. For most of my life I was using my sense of humor as a blanket to pull over my head, like a child does when he is in bed alone in the dark, so the monsters don't get him. Now I use my sense of humor as a transformational tool to confront my monsters.

My experiences revealed to me a whole new way of viewing what I thought a sense of humor was. The profound effect it had on so many people compelled me to investigate in more detail this phenomenon we call our sense of humor. My investigation led to the discovery of a force that can lift us up and guide us to move forward, even in the midst of the most challenging circumstances. I call this force my *humor being*.

High Points to Remember

⚘ Set goals for yourself, follow your dreams, and pray for guidance. But don't expect immediate results or instant gratification. The most important thing to remember is to enjoy yourself along the way. Dare to laugh off your disappointments and setbacks.

⚘ Take one step at a time. When you skip steps you negate the process. You have not accomplished anything if you did not experience the process.

⚘ Nothing in life is wasted if you learn from it. Every step forward and backward is necessary to prepare you to receive the gift when it's revealed to you.

Chapter One
What is a Humor Being?

*It was the awakening and nurturing of my
humor being more than anything else that
guided me through my pain.*

I have discovered that a sense of humor is
more than just the ability to laugh. Laughter is a by-product of humor, a very important by-product, but still just a part of the many wonderful healing qualities that a sense of humor has to offer.

The dictionary says the word *sense* means perception or awareness; and correct reasoning; or sound judgment. The word *humor* means turn of mind, to soothe temper or mood, or the mental quality that produces absurd or joyful ideas. So we can say that a sense of humor is to have perception or to be aware that you have a mental quality to turn your mind or mood to produce joyful or absurd ideas that can soothe your very being by correct reasoning and sound judgment.

All of the successful and happy people I know personally or have studied throughout history had to overcome adversity of some kind. Inventors, discoverers, entrepreneurs, actors, sports figures, artists, and great minds of all kinds had to face major challenges and defy insurmountable odds on their journeys toward success. But they all had an ongoing optimism to move forward. Each of them had an awareness, or perception, to turn their moods to produce joyful ideas, an ability to soothe their very being by correct reasoning and sound judgment. This awareness or perception, as I have already stated, is by definition a sense of humor. The initiative and proficiency by which we utilize it, however, comes from what I call our *humor being*. Let me explain.

One of the biggest misconceptions we have about ourselves when times are challenging is when we say the all too common phrase, *"I'm only human."* This statement is not only a limiting belief, but an injustice to our very existence. We are not only human beings; we are also spiritual beings. In fact, we are spiritual beings experiencing our lives in a human body or shell. When the body dies the spirit lives on.

Within the body or shell there also lives our *humor being*. Our *humor being* is of the spirit—our higher self. It always comes from a state of love. In fact, it is love. It is a part of our intuition that simply knows a sense of humor can help us acquire the success, happiness, and inner peace we all desire. Then it shows us how to use it accordingly.

It is the *humor being* within all of us that helps us see the brighter alternative to a potentially negative situation. It is there to help us view and deal with our challenges, even our tragedies, from a healthier perspective. The *humor being* within you has the power to lift you up and give you hope to move forward when it seems your world has run out of saviors. The *humor being* within you is a part of you that can help bring the real you back to yourself.

As a child I acquired many fears and negative labels about myself. As you will see in later chapters, my experiences with adults, teachers, and my peers led me to believe I was never good enough or smart enough. I was programmed with many limiting and negative beliefs. Unfortunately, these beliefs became my reality. As a result, I kept experiencing and reliving the same mistakes and failures over and over again. I was never aware that I had options. For most of my life I needed the approval of others to validate that I was good enough. Their opinions, especially people with authority, meant more to me than my own. My constant need for their approval totally voided any chance for me to choose a better way.

That's what happens when you are consumed by fear. You don't or can't exercise your right to choose. You surrender your power and feel stuck. I have seen too many people drowning in hopelessness. There are far too many people who accept their plight and all of the garbage that life throws at them every day, never knowing that they have the power to choose and change.

It was the awakening and nurturing of my *humor being*, more than anything else, which guided me through my pain. My *humor being* showed me that no matter what happened to me in the past, whatever will happen in the future, or what is happening now, in the present, I have a choice on how to deal with it. My *humor being* showed me that my sense of humor is my sense of perspective. It's a choice we all have on how to deal with the challenges and difficulties that life throws at us every day.

Truly successful people attempt to understand the mystery and drama in life, but they also give their *humor being* freedom to explore and to acknowledge life's hilarity, absurdities, and incomprehensibilities at the same time. It is the combination of the two points of view that leads towards a healthy existence.

This book, in part, is about how my *humor being* helped me acquire the faith and the right frame of consciousness I needed to overcome my fears and to follow my heart's desire. This book is also about the power of choice, and how a sense of humor can connect you to your higher power.

My attempt is to show you that no matter what challenges life might bestow upon you throughout your journey, it is the thought you have about the challenge that will ultimately determine the quality of your success, happiness, and inner peace. This is where your *humor being* can help you in miraculous ways. Humor short-circuits negative thoughts and emotions before they get programmed as emotional havoc.

Through my story and through the stories of others, you will see how the powers of humor, hope, and love work individually, and together as one force, to change your perception of challenging and difficult times. As it states in *A Course in Miracles*, whenever any experience in our lives transforms us from a state of fear and chaos to a state of love and peace, a miracle has been performed.

The following story is a good example of how my *humor being* helped a family during a most difficult time.

A SPECIAL GIFT

It was the first week of April 1992, and the third night of a week's stay at a comedy club in Columbus, Ohio. The manager of the club approached me before the show and handed me a letter that was addressed to me. I took the letter and walked into the lounge to read it.

It was from a Susie Murray. She was thanking me for making her nephew, David, and the rest of her family laugh at a time in their lives when even a smile appeared to be obsolete. She explained that David had cancer of the stomach and was getting progressively worse. He was only twenty-four years old, and he was the only son of her sister, Rosie. To see David laugh, after everything he had been through, gave all of them a sense of hope that life could still be enjoyed on some level, even in the midst of so much physical and emotional duress.

I stopped reading for a moment. The sincerity of her words affected me greatly. I felt uplifted and worthy that I was able to help in some way. Yet, I felt sympathy and compassion for the pain this family must have been experiencing. I continued reading. Susie stated that the day after they saw my show David was walking around the house reciting parts of my act. She said it was a joy to see him in such good spirits. She then requested to purchase one of the T-shirts that I sell at the end of my show. She said how wonderful and ironic it was that I was giving the proceeds from the T-shirt sales to The National Children's Cancer Society.

That's when it hit me. I had met David the night he and his family came to see me perform. He was the young man who had approached me after the show when I was selling T-shirts. I remembered there were people everywhere. David approached me with some hesitation, shook my hand and said, *"Thanks for making me laugh. I don't have any money on me now, but I think it's wonderful that the proceeds go to The Children's Cancer Society."* He told me that he had cancer. I asked him how he was dealing with it. He said with a smile, *"Well, I can still laugh."* I was very

16

impressed by his attitude. I turned around to reach into the box to pull out a T-shirt for him. When I turned around, he was gone.

The next day I called Susie at the number she had written at the bottom of the letter. I told her I had a Steve Rizzo T-shirt for David. I also asked if it would be all right if I talked with him. She said he would love to hear from me.

I called David the next day and we bonded immediately. We talked about what he did for a living and what he enjoyed doing most. But he seemed especially intrigued at what I did for a living. He wanted to know what it was like to live the life of a comedian. We had quite a few laughs during our conversation. He asked so many questions that I thought I was being interviewed by *People* magazine. We ended the conversation by me telling him to have faith and keep laughing. I also told him I was sending him a Steve Rizzo A-FOR-GET-ABOUT-IT T-shirt and some videos from some of my TV specials.

I continued to keep in touch with David and his family. Rosie told me David wouldn't take off my T-shirt, and that he constantly watched my videos. She said David had my act down with such perfection that if I ever decided I didn't want to perform one night, he could take my place.

On April 26th I received a letter from Rosie. David's condition was getting worse. He was in a lot of pain, and the doctors had confirmed that the cancer had spread to his liver. He was to be admitted to the hospital for a week to undergo more tests and heavy doses of chemotherapy. She thanked me once again for being a part of David's life.

On May 5th Rosie left a message with my answering service. David was in critical condition and getting weaker by the minute. I dialed the number that was a direct line to David's hospital room. Rosie answered the phone and told me he was too weak to talk and was not taking calls from anyone. I told her I understood and to please tell David I was asking for him.

Somehow, David knew it was me on the phone and motioned to his mom that he wanted to talk. He was too weak to hold the phone, so Rosie held it for him. I knew he was in pain and heavily sedated. I told him not to talk, just to listen. To be honest, I don't remember exactly what I said, but it was something about a typical hectic day in the life of Steve Rizzo. I somehow sensed the urgency to tell David that I would stay in touch with his family and that my prayers were with him and them.

On May 6th, only hours after our conversation, I received a call from David's stepfather. David had passed away.

A few days later, Rosie told me that she didn't know what I had said to David in our last conversation, but something I said had given him the last of many smiles he had put on his face since our paths crossed. She couldn't thank me enough. Then she said something that totally took me by surprise; David was being buried with my T-shirt clutched in his hands.

When I hung up the phone I was overwhelmed by a wave of emotions. Not just because of David's death, but because of the profound affect I had had on his life.

I had only met David once. How and why did I have such an impact? I was only doing my job. I'm supposed to make people laugh. I didn't have any idea as to how or why I was affecting people on such a personal level. But I was; that much was certain.

Below are the words on a plaque I received from David's family:

To Steven Rizzo

You had no way of knowing
What your simple words would do
They put a smile on his face
And kept him from feeling blue

You had no way of knowing
You made his world seem bright
You gave him a sense of being
And a friendship he knew was right

You had no way of knowing
Your laughter was so needed
It brought him joy and pleasure
When he really felt defeated

You had no way of knowing
How much we needed you
But somehow you always knew
Just exactly what to do

Steve, thanks for all your kindness, caring and deep concern for Dave and all of the family. You will always be in our hearts and thoughts, not only as a friend but also as a very important person in our lives.

Keep Them Laughing!
The David R. Davies Family

Not only did my *humor being* lift David's spirit and help him embrace his death and overcome his fear, but it also lifted his family's spirits and helped them embrace his death and overcome their fears as well. To all of us, the entire experience was a wonderful healing process. It was a return to love.

In other letters that followed Rosie and Susie told me I was the answer to their prayers and a hero to a twenty-four-year-old boy. They told me I was David's ray of hope; that extra touch that family sometimes just can't give. They thanked God for the gift I have and urged me to never stop making people laugh.

Many times throughout our lives we are drawn to people who are in need of our assistance. I believe we all have a special gift to give. Don't ignore a call for help. Reaching out to someone who is suffering, even a total stranger, is more than just a nice thing to do. It's our obligation. It is a part of what makes us feel connected. The reward is in the giving itself. It's an exhilarating feeling of completeness and total peace.

Sometimes all it takes is your willingness to listen, or to show that you care. At times, all that is needed is a hug or a word of encouragement. In the case of David and his family, it was my simple ability to ease their pain and lift their spirits through the power of one of God's greatest gifts, a sense of humor.

Humor was the catalyst that brought us together. It is a bond that can bring all people together. Humor has a magical way of breaking down barriers and making people realize that we are all the same in God's eyes.

The real miracle, however, is the special friendship and growth that evolved from reaching out and taking an extra step to help a family in need; a family I didn't even know. Our friendship continues. My wife and I still keep in touch with Rosie; Susie; David's stepfather, Steve; and Susie's husband, Mike (alias Sparky). Whenever I'm in the Columbus area, I'm invited over for a wonderful day of Rosie's home cooking, Susie's famous carrot cake, great conversation, and laughter! Lots of laughter!

HIGH POINTS TO REMEMBER

☙ Our *humor being* is of the spirit—our higher self. It always comes from a state of love. In fact, it is love.

☙ It is the *humor being* within all of us that helps us to see the brighter alternative to a potentially negative situation.

☙ Truly successful people attempt to understand the mystery and drama in life, but they also give their *humor being* freedom to explore and to acknowledge life's hilarity, absurdity, and incomprehensibilities at the same time. It is the combination of the two points of view that leads towards a healthy existence.

Chapter Two
Way Beyond Comedy

I noticed the more I utilized my sense of humor as a tool to help me deal with my challenges, the more it became a part of who I was, and the more emotionally balanced I became.

Quite often people come up to me and say, *"Steve"* (because that's my name), *"what's one of the main characteristics that separates a comedian from everyone else?"* I simply respond that it's the way a comedian looks at life. A comedian views life and all of its obstacles, absurdities, tragedies, mistakes, incomprehensibilities, and embarrassing moments from a humorous perspective. When comedians look at life this way, they're not negating the seriousness of the subject matter, they're just looking at life from a different perspective. It's a healthier perspective—*it's the humor perspective.*

Let me share with you how I discovered the power of my *humor being*; which was one of the key factors that motivated me to leave stand-up comedy and move on to the speaking forum.

Following a comedy performance I would feel this surge of positive energy flow through my body. This energy surge gave me the confidence that I could achieve and accomplish anything I set my mind to do. Sometimes I would go back to my hotel room and write in my journal or write new material. It seemed that my creative juices flowed from me, into the pen, and onto the paper. Other times I would go out with a group of people, have wonderful conversation, laugh and have fun. The point is, whatever I did I was totally void of all negative thoughts. And my problems, whatever they were at the time, somehow seemed manageable. I was living in the moment and enjoying every minute of it.

Initially I thought the reason for these power surges was because I was feeding my ego. You know, standing ovations, signing autographs, and people wanting to be around me. Although all of these things made me feel good, I knew there had to be more to it than that. Then one night after a comedy performance it hit me. It was at a time in my life when I was at an all-time low. I was either in or very close to a state of depression. All of the old fears and limiting beliefs that I thought I had conquered were back, haunting me again. It took everything I had to muster up enough energy and courage to step onto the stage that night. I remember thinking how ironic life is. There I was, ready to make a sold-out crowd of over five hundred people laugh, when what I really wanted to do was tell them how much life sucked. Much to my surprise, I was able to do both.

In spite of my problems—in fact it was because of my problems—I had one of the most spectacular performances of my career. I was on stage for more than two hours, and the crowd wanted more. When I finally stepped off the stage the euphoria hit me with more intensity than ever before. I remember saying to myself: *This is way beyond comedy.* I actually felt invincible. I felt a presence in me that radiated confidence and hope. I was in a complete state of love, and it was because I had allowed my *humor being* to take me there.

It was then that I discovered the real reason I got the power surge of positive energy. When I'm up on stage, I am in a totally different state of mind. I'm in a place where my problems and the world's problems are viewed in a different light.

That night I did more than my usual act. I let my *humor being* loose and allowed my higher self to take control. I talked about my world and how it was falling apart. I even talked about some painful experiences from my past. I literally laughed off my frustrations, pain, negative labels and innermost fears. I vented my anger in a constructive way and the crowd loved it. It was like therapy, with two major differences: I had fun and I didn't have to pay for it.

A few days after my performance, I began to reflect on what had transpired on stage that night. Without my knowledge, the owner of the club had recorded my entire performance. When I listened to the tape, I was amazed at what I heard. It felt strange to listen to myself ramble on about my personal history in such a way. I was never afraid to speak my mind, but if I didn't know any better I would have thought I was possessed or that someone had injected me with some kind of serum that made me reveal parts of myself that were never touched before. I now know it was really my *humor being* exposing my fears for what they were. Through laughter I was able to understand that my negative labels and the fears that belonged to them didn't have to formulate my reality if I didn't want them to.

I also came to understand that the reason the people in the audience enjoyed themselves so much was because they were laughing at extensions of themselves. My stories and the humor behind them helped these people view their own personal problems from a healthier perspective. In other words, our *humor beings* were connected. We were feeding off of each other.

That's what humor does. It makes us realize that we are all the same in God's eyes. We have the same fears,

pains, and heartaches. We just have different
It doesn't matter who you are, what you do,
money you make. It doesn't matter if yo
white, male or female, rich or poor, conservative or liberal,
or homosexual or heterosexual. We all make mistakes. We
all have our successes and failures. We all have good times
and bad times. Humor just has a way of ironing out the
wrinkles. Humor helps us embrace who we really are and
gives us enough peace to live with it.

The next time you're being entertained by a comedian,
listen to the underlying statement that is so often hidden
within the laughter. Many comedians are venting their
phobias and innermost fears. Some talk about the pain
and hassles of divorce and their inability to stay in relationships. Many discuss their addictions to drugs, alcohol,
gambling, and sex. Others find levity in their physical or
mental handicaps. Some even describe the abuse they had
to endure while growing up. As I said at the beginning of
this chapter, they are not negating the seriousness of the
subject matter. They are choosing to view their pain from
a healthier perspective.

One could certainly argue that if humor is so healing,
then why didn't it heal the three comedy greats, Lenny
Bruce, John Belushi and Chris Farley? I suggest that
Lenny, John and Chris were hiding behind the humor.
They used the comedy arena as an escape. In other words,
these three extremely talented funnymen were using

humor as a mask to cover up their problems. This is something worth mentioning because some comedians as well as some people in all walks of life do this. Hiding behind laughter can be dangerous. It can give a false impression not only to others but also to oneself that everything is OK, when in reality they're living with a lifetime of unresolved pain, fear, and anger.

When you are unable to face what's eating at your inner core, you run the risk of living a lie. Unfortunately, laughter is a wonderful, easy way to cover up the lie. Those who feed the lie with laughter are usually the ones that everybody loves. They're the life of the party. They're always cracking jokes and they will go out of their way to make people laugh.

We all know people like this. They're the "Goodtime Charlies" who don't seem to have a care in the world. Quite often, "Goodtime Charlies" consume a great deal of alcohol and drugs. It helps them hide behind the laughter. One could say that laughter in itself is a drug, especially to a "Goodtime Charlie". They partake in it for the high that it gives. They depend on it for the same reason people do cocaine, shoot heroin or use any other drug. It helps them to temporarily escape. Unfortunately, when used this way, laughter has no healing effect or medicinal purpose at all. In fact, it just adds more fuel to the lie.

The problem with living a lie is that every time the truth tries to reveal itself, the ego jumps in and says, "It's *okay! You're okay! Forget that empty feeling. You're not afraid. You're not angry or insecure! You're in total control! You have money. You're a great success. Everybody loves you! What else could you possibly need? I'll tell you what you need. You need more drugs, more alcohol! That's what you need. That's it, now crack a few jokes. Ya feel funnier already, don't ya? Go ahead make 'em laugh! There now, you see. I told you! Don't you feel better?"*

Lenny Bruce, John Belushi, and Chris Farley, were extremely talented. Each had their own unique gifts to give to the world. As funny as they were, I believe that none of them was in tune with their *humor being*. I'm not saying that they were unhappy or died prematurely because of this. However, it's only when we confront the liar within us and stand face-to-face with our demons that we can expect the healing process to begin.

It's obvious that Lenny, John, and Chris were unable to confront the liar within. All three were stuck in high gear on the fast lane of life. They didn't see that the lights were turning red. They didn't heed the warning signals. It's impossible to heal if you don't allow yourself to slow down and acknowledge that something is wrong. Lenny, John, and Chris had the tools to better themselves. (We all do!) They just didn't use them.

I can't help but wonder what might have happened if they were able to connect with their *humor beings*. What would the outcome have been had they been able to use their incredible humor talents to confront their fears, instead of running from them? Humor isn't the only way. It's simply a way. A wonderful example on how humor can help you face your truth and confront your fears is in the following story.

Emotional Self-Defense

One Saturday night, years ago, I was performing at The Comedy Store in Los Angeles. I was backstage conversing with a fellow comedian named Steve. We were discussing what a trip it was to make people laugh, and better yet, get paid for it. We agreed that the power of laughter has many medicinal purposes. I suggested that since we were responsible for making people laugh, that would make us "Humor Healing Technicians."

The conversation took on a more serious tone when Steve told me he was HIV positive. I asked how he was dealing with it. He said, *"Watch me."*

"What?"

He said, *"I'm going on before you. Watch my set."*

I went to the back of the room and stood by some other comedians. The room was sold-out—standing room only. Steve was introduced. What transpired within the next 20 minutes totally blew my mind. His entire routine was on the HIV virus. His opening line was: *"Hi, I'm Steve and I'm HIV positive. Don't be concerned, Naomi Judd was diagnosed with chronic Hepatitis C.*

The good news is that we are going to form a duo and call ourselves Sick and Tired."

Steve had an incredible ability to use humor as a tool. His *humor being* glowed that night. His comic timing was exceptional; equaled only by the powerful message that was interwoven in and around the laughter. He even found humor in the many side effects that occurred from all the different medication he was taking. There were over five hundred people in that room and Steve had them all in the palm of his hand. He made them realize how healing laughter can be and how precious life truly is. I remember saying to another comedian, *"This guy is making people laugh about one of the biggest challenges to face this planet."*

Later that evening our conversation continued. I told Steve that what he did on stage took courage and was absolutely incredible. He smiled and said, *"Thank you, but do you really want to hear the good news?"*

"Yeah," I said.

"My white blood count went up phenomenally, ever since I chose to deal with this challenge with humor."

I stood there with my mouth open, searching for the proper words. Finally I said, *"That's incredible."*

Later in his career, Steve starred in his own HBO special entitled, "HIV." He now has a following. There are people who are HIV positive who claim that Steve's humor and message help them embrace their challenges.

One very important point must be made. Steve was not laughing *at* his challenge. We know there is nothing funny about the HIV virus. Nor was he hiding behind the laughter. What he was doing, however, was allowing his *humor being* to laugh off the fear that represented the challenge. This is something I believe Lenny Bruce, John Belushi, and Chris Farley were unable to do.

Laughing in the face of fear eventually helped Steve confront his challenge. When he confronted his fear he gradually began to understand where it was coming from and why it was controlling his life. Understanding always leads to compassion and compassion leads to the ultimate, unconditional love.

The most incredible accomplishment my friend Steve is making is that he is letting people know they have the power within themselves to view their own personal challenges from the same perspective. He reminds us that we all have a *humor being* within us, but it's up to us whether we choose to use it or not.

One of the greatest accomplishments I made is when I realized I didn't have to wait to be the comedian onstage to deal with my fear and anger. I discovered that my *humor being* is just as effective off stage as it is on. Gradually, I made a conscious effort to find the humor in my challenging and stressful situations. In time, I noticed that my problems didn't seem that big. My anger didn't last as long and my fears never had a chance to overwhelm me when I stopped and said out loud that I had a choice on how to deal with it.

Telling yourself that you have a choice, and believing that your thoughts are your life puts your challenges into focus. It's then you are aware of the consequences that will eventually follow.

Even a little levity can help change your perception of a particular problem. I noticed that the more I utilized my sense of humor as a tool to help me deal with my challenges, the more it became a part of who I was and the more emotionally balanced I became. You could say that dealing with life's stresses and challenges from a humor perspective is emotional self-defense—which is very much akin with the principals and theories of the martial arts. Let me explain.

My friend Jeff has a black belt degree in karate. Through years of practice and repetitious training he has conditioned his mind and body to respond automatically against physical attack with a series of self-defense moves consisting of kicks, punches, blocks, and throws.

One night at a club someone attacked Jeff by surprise and punched him in the back of the head. Fortunately for Jeff the punch didn't make full contact. Without even thinking, Jeff automatically went into his defense stance, blocked the next punch that was thrown, threw two punches of his own, and hurled his assailant through the air and onto the floor.

When it was over Jeff sat down in a chair, brought his hand to his face and said, *"Wow! I just got into a fight!"* He said he didn't have to think about blocking the next punch or when or how to punch back. He said it just happened. That's conditioning. His mind and body worked together to respond with automatic reflex to keep him from harm's way—to protect his physical self.

In karate one is constantly practicing their *katas*, which are a series of physical moves such as kicks, punches, jumps, and throws. These *katas* condition the student to respond and react effectively in the event of physical attack.

If you make a conscious effort every day to see the humor in the events that attack your emotional well-being you will be practicing your emotional *kata*. Slowly but surely, you will reprogram your brain subconsciously to the point that when a major emotional attack occurs you will automatically respond to it with more ease.

Humor is your natural defense mechanism. It's a prescription from your higher self to cure the madness that attacks you from day to day. To deny yourself the right to find humor in the midst of all the madness is like denying yourself treatment that can cure an illness.

High Points to Remember

❧ We all make mistakes. We all have our good times and bad times. Humor has a way of ironing out the wrinkles.

❧ Allow your *humor being* to laugh off the fear that represents your greatest challenge. Laughing in the face of fear puts you in control.

❧ Make a conscious effort every day to see the humor in the events that attack your emotional well-being. In time, you will have reprogrammed yourself to the point that when a major challenge occurs, you will be able to deal with it more easily.

Chapter Three
Enjoy and Be Happy

Contrary to what many people think, happiness is not determined by outside circumstances. Rather it is determined by how we view our circumstances.

When I speak to groups I usually ask for a show of hands of how many people get upset when they're in a traffic jam. Without fail, almost everyone raises his or her hand. Then I ask why they don't laugh when they're stuck in traffic. At this point about half the audience is giving me the Archie Bunker look, as if to say, *"Well, that's because it's not funny there, Meathead."* or *"Jeez, where did they get this dingbat from?"*

What most people aren't aware of is that the mood they are in as a result of a traffic jam can determine the mood they're going to be in for the rest of the day. This doesn't sound very promising, considering that your mood affects your quality of happiness.

What if you have a business meeting scheduled or an important decision has to be made? Maybe it's your anniversary or your child's birthday. The point is that your mood, good or bad, has the power to affect the outcome of everything you do. So, instead of getting angry, why not laugh when you're in traffic or when someone is getting on your nerves or when the workload is too much? Why not laugh when the kids are out of control or when you're waiting in a long line at the store or bank? If your answer is, *"Because it's not funny"* then my question right back to you is, *"Why don't you make it funny?"*

When I'm stuck in traffic I know that I have a choice. I am also aware (through experience) that certain choices will infringe upon my happiness. I figure if I have a choice, I'm going to do anything within my power to keep myself from getting in a bad mood. I can either let the situation control my emotions or I can do something to nip these negative emotions in the bud before they blossom into emotional havoc.

What I usually do is something you might call crazy! Quite often, when I'm stuck in traffic, I turn into the lion from *The Wizard of Oz*. Why not? Everyone else is angry, their blood pressure is boiling, and they're beeping their horns and cursing at each other. Not me. I'm behind the wheel of my car, motioning the other drivers (as the Cowardly Lion) *"Grrah, grraha, aha, aha, aha. I wanna go home! I wanna go home! I don't like traffic. I'm afraid of it! Ahaa, ahaa, ha!"*

If you don't think this is funny, then you should check out the expressions on everyone's faces as I slowly inch by their car. I could only imagine what they're thinking or saying. *"Don't look at him, honey!" "Lock the door, and look straight ahead!" "He's a pervert!" "He's got a New York license plate!" "Look straight ahead and don't look at him! He's probably naked from the waist down! Don't look at him!"*

You might think I'm crazy. So might everyone in traffic. But at least I know I'm not going home to my family or meeting with a customer in a bad mood. In fact, I'm in a good mood. Why? Because I changed my state of mind. I was able to go from a potentially bad mood to a good mood by connecting with my *humor being*. The good news is that you have the power to do this—or something like it.

Whenever a situation is about to infringe upon your happiness, it is essential to your emotional well-being that you know you have a choice. You always have a choice! You can let the situation control you or you can take control of the situation.

Things don't always have to go your way or be right before you can be happy. Contrary to what many people think, happiness is not determined by outside circumstances; rather it is determined by how we view our circumstances. We don't always have to control people and events, but we do have the power to be happy. The key is to know you have a choice on how to deal with adversity.

John Lennon once said, "Life is what happens to you while you're busy making other plans." What a profound statement. It's how we perceive and act upon what happens that gives us access towards the happiness we all desire.

Our natural state of being is one of inner peace. When you let outside circumstances determine your happiness, your natural state of peace deteriorates. When this happens inner peace is replaced with a sense of being cheated and that the world and everyone in it is out to get you. This is what I call the *"Why me?"* syndrome.

> *"Why is it that every time I get in line at the grocery store there is a price check?"*
>
> *"Why do I have to be sick now?"*
>
> *"Why can't I get a break?"*

This type of thinking is very controlling and leads to a lack of confidence in yourself and a lack of trust in the process of life. As a result, your enjoyment and appreciation of all of the good and beauty that life has to offer gets distorted. This leaves you with a twisted and unhappy existence.

In order for you to choose happiness you must understand that you are the creator of your thoughts. Thoughts don't just happen to you. They're something you create. When something bad or upsetting happens, it's not the situation that makes you unhappy. It's your thoughts about the situation that cause you to feel a certain way.

Let me give you an example. My wife and I were in the process of purchasing a house that was built in 1918. We knew at first glance that this was the house of our dreams. It had everything we've always wanted in a house. We knew a lot of work needed to be done, but still we were both very excited and enthusiastic about our new venture. In fact, fixing it up was part of the fun.

One morning however, I woke up feeling very disturbed and unsure about all of the work that needed to be done. All of these thoughts were going through my brain. *Did I choose the right contractor for the job? Should I knock out all of the plaster walls and replace them with sheetrock? Should I put the sheetrock over the plaster? If I don't gut out the walls, I'll never know what kind of wiring, plumbing or insulation it has. This could be a fire hazard! What if the whole house needs to be re-wired? What if they take longer than they said? What if they damage the foundation? What will I do if the contractor gets sick or dies halfway through the job? This is costing me more than I thought! How do I know I was quoted the right price? Sure, I can afford it, but maybe I should have put my money into a new house?*

Do you see what I was doing to myself? That particular morning I was very close to turning my dream house into a house of horrors. I allowed myself to create a thought pattern that was causing a negative emotional response. My emotional response was setting off an unhealthy physiological response. My heart was racing, my stomach was tight. I just didn't feel right. These physiological side effects were causing me to think more negatively, which in turn was causing me to feel more emotionally disturbed, and so on.

It's a vicious negative cycle that can create disastrous results. I was actually beginning to believe that this house was not worth the trouble. This web of negativity I was caught up in, kept me from seeing the beauty this house had to offer.

Lucky for me, I was aware of what I was doing to myself. I knew I was creating an unhealthy reality. If I kept reviewing these negative scenarios over and over, I could have convinced myself that the entire project was going to be more trouble than it's worth.

One of my lifetime goals is to stay at peace with my negative and neurotic moments. I don't try to fight them or pretend they're not there. But rather, I embrace them. I've come to realize that they too are a part of who I am. And, they will probably be with me forever. This acceptance of the dark sides of myself is very healthy. The difference now is that I find it amusing how they keep popping up and try to prevail in my world. And, when I allow myself the freedom to laugh at them and what they're trying to do, they actually begin to lose their power. It's as if I'm saying to them, *"I know you're there, and I know what you're trying to do. You've had your few moments of glory. But now, get lost! I have a life to enjoy!"*

So remember, just one negative incident first thing in

the morning can cause a snowball effect. It can regulate everything you do throughout the day. It can control your energy, your enthusiasm and your spirit. Just one negative thought first thing in the morning can take a dream filled with hope and blow it to pieces.

You have probably heard the saying, "Your brain is like a computer." Well, in a way it is, and your thoughts are like data. Whatever thoughts get programmed into your computer will determine the information that is registered back to you. And the emotional state that you are in as your brain is being programmed will play a major role in determining the information that is registered back to you. For example, if you are in a reckless, panicked, and emotional state and you are programming your computer with ...

"Why is this happening to me?"

"I knew this would happen!"

"I can never win!"

"I'm just not cut out for this!"

"Why does everyone else have what I want?"

"What an idiot I am!"

Your brain will have no choice but to give you the information that was programmed. For example:

"This is happening because you're a loser!"

"You can never win because you're not smart enough!"

"Everyone else has what you want because they made the right choice."

"You always make the wrong choice!"

It's obvious that if you allow yourself to go on emotional binges filled with negative thoughts you will be setting yourself up for failure, chaos, and unhappiness.

The good news is that you have a choice as to what thoughts you want programmed. I urge you to choose wisely, because the thoughts that you have about a particular challenge will lead to the outcome of your destiny.

This is where even a little levity can be of tremendous assistance. Viewing any challenge from a humorous perspective helps feed your brain with positive data, aiding in a healthier, more productive, and happier life.

Let's break down step-by-step how a negative process formulates. We will use my story about being stuck in traffic. I'm using traffic as an example because it's an experience we can all relate to. Note, however, that the same process takes place with all negative situations.

Follow me on this and notice how one negative thought can very easily spring out of control. Let's say I'm on my way to the airport and I'm stuck in a massive traffic jam. I look around and notice that the Long Island Expressway looks like a parking lot. Cars are inching their way all around me. Then it happens. I shake my head and blurt out the words, *"Here we go again!"* That's it! That's all it takes! I have just cracked open the door to the negative zone. And it opened the moment I shook my head in disgust and said the magic words, *"Here we go again!"* Now I am vulnerable and defenseless. And, without me even being aware of what's happening, the door opens wider, leaving an opening for an avalanche of similar thoughts to reap havoc. *"This is absolutely ridiculous!" "Every morning it's the same thing!" "What do I have to do, get up five hours earlier just to get to the airport on time?!"*

Eventually I take the experience to another level. I mean, it's bad enough that I'm stuck in traffic. Now I actually believe that everyone on the road is out just to annoy me. *"Look at this guy, what an idiot!" Where did he get his license, at the bottom of a Cracker Jack box?! Why is that every time I drive, I'm surrounded by idiots?!"*

It's obvious that the wrath of negativity is showing me no mercy. Not only is the door to the Negative Zone open, but now I've allowed myself to enter. At this point, I actually start believing that every aspect of my life is in total chaos! *"This is ridiculous! Oh great, it's snowing! Now I'll never get to the airport on time! Even if I do, my flight will probably will be cancelled or delayed! I'll never make my connection! What a way to make a living! If that's what you want to call it!"*

Now my emotional state is just a bit out of whack. And my entire physiology is just a tad tense. All of this, of course, adds to this near-hysterical outburst. Here is where I go for the kill and destroy any chance I have to get a grip on this exaggerated experience. *"Why do I go through all of this aggravation? I make all this money for what? So, the IRS can take half! And half of the half that I have left goes right back into my business! What good is making money if you can't enjoy it? I spend most of my time in traffic, airports, airplanes, and hotels! This is absolutely insane!"* (Yes it is. I am emotionally drained just by *writing* this.)

It's clear that I'm setting myself up for unhappiness. I'm allowing my *thoughts* to lead me to *believe* that my life isn't working. I've actually convinced myself that I'm miserable. This, of course, is causing me to have a really bad *attitude*. This bad *attitude*, in turn, is leading me to *feel* victimized, hopeless and drained. This will no doubt direct me to take *actions* that will not be conducive to being productive, which could very possibly lead to an *outcome* I'll regret. Doesn't sound very promising does it? And it all started with one *thought*.

When I turn my *humor being* loose, however, and allow myself to act like the lion from *The Wizard Of Oz* (or something else out of the ordinary), I'm not only nipping the negative thoughts in the bud, but I'm changing my state of mind.

It is also important to note that I've made a conscious decision to change my experience of being in traffic. I'm having fun in what could have been a negative situation. As a result, my energy is up and I have the emotional benefits to deal with the challenges of the day.

Right now I know some of you are saying, *"But I don't think I could allow myself to act like the lion from* The Wizard of Oz. *I don't think I can do something crazy or out of the ordinary. What if there are people in the car with me?"*

Well, great! This can be a wonderful opportunity to make them feel good as well! All I'm asking you to do is to try it. What a wonderful trait to acquire. What a wonderful trait to instill in your family—especially your children. If children understood the power of their thoughts at an early age and knew they always have healthy alternatives on how to deal with life's stresses, they would have an incredible head start as they reached adulthood.

Whenever you use your *humor being* in any stressful situation, make a mental note to yourself as to how it helped you to regain control. Make sure you know it changed your experience.

The key to nipping any negative thought in the bud is to recognize that you nipped it in the bud. It is important that you understood the process of how you did it.

Often people regain some sort of mental or emotional health by nipping or dropping negative thoughts, but they lack the understanding as to how it was done. So the next time they are subjected to negative thinking they will fall victim to the same pattern.

When you are consciously aware, however, as to how you took control of a negative situation and if you remind yourself that it was your *humor being* that helped, you have empowered yourself. Then you can choose the same method or something similar the next time and the time after that—until it becomes part of who you are.

It is important to remember that your brain cannot distinguish true from false, or right from wrong. It only takes in data.

If you consistently feed yourself, or if you allow others to feed you with thoughts that you're not good enough or that you are cursed and the world is out to get you, you will create a very unpleasant belief system. This belief system will eventually cause you to take certain actions that will be counter-productive to your success and happiness on all levels of your life.

You must constantly remind yourself that your habitual thought patterns will formulate your reality. When you come to the realization that you can choose the thoughts you want programmed you will then harbor more positive feelings about yourself and take positive actions.

I Won't Be Happy Until...

Many people convince themselves that things have to happen or not happen in their lives in order for them to be happy. If you assure yourself that certain conditions must be met before you can be happy, then you will never experience true happiness. At best, if you're lucky, you might feel fleeting moments of happiness.

Some people say they only need to get up in the morning in order to be happy. Others let outside conditions, such as the weather or a traffic jam determine their happiness. Some people say they have to be married and have children in order to be happy. Many say they have to look good and feel one hundred percent healthy in order to be happy. There are those who let the opinions of others determine their happiness. And then, there are people who believe that it will take an abundance of wealth or fame in order for them to enjoy life.

If it is true that your happiness is determined by what you believe has to happen or not happen in your life, then it is fair to say that if you could change your beliefs you could regulate the quality of your happiness. How do you change your beliefs? Yes, that's right. By changing your way of thinking. Remember, your thoughts create your beliefs.

People in all walks of life experience unhappiness because they are unable to shake off unfortunate circumstances from their past or they worry endlessly about what will happen in the future. This type of thinking keeps them from enjoying the moment. Author Mihaly Csikszentmihalyi says that, *"True happiness comes from relishing the moment, from living in the moment; not in obtaining some distant goal or consuming material wealth."*

I believe one of the biggest injustices we can ever do to ourselves is to put our happiness on hold. How many times have you said things like: *"I'll be happy when I get married." "I'll be happy when I get divorced." "I won't be happy until I find someone to love." "If I had more money I would be happy." "I won't be happy until I achieve my goals." "I'll be happy when the job is finished." "I'll be happy when the bills are paid." "I'll be happy when I move." "I'll enjoy myself when it stops raining." "I'll be happy when the world changes." "I'll be happy when I graduate." "I'll be happy when the weekend is here."*

If any of the above sounds familiar, you are cheating yourself. You are missing out on an important element of life. What element? To simply enjoy yourself during the process!

What process? The processes of obtaining that house or job. The process of achieving your goals. The process of obtaining more. The process of trying to overcome a major challenge. Life is a process. It's one thing after another. Don't ignore your right to enjoy the process. There is just too much good stuff for you not to be happy, even when things aren't going the way you want them to.

Furthermore, this type of thinking prevents happiness from entering your life. You are actually convincing yourself that your happiness is dependent upon outside circumstances, that certain things must happen or not happen for you to be happy. This mindset stays with you and will keep you from ever enjoying the moment.

If you keep telling yourself that you won't be happy

until... you won't be happy at all. Here is something to think about. What if *until* never comes? What if you don't achieve that goal or dream? What if you don't get that house for another five or ten years?

Our greatest treasures are the memories we gather as we journey through life. You won't have many fond memories if you put your happiness on hold. Once you get to where you wanted to go, once the journey is over and the goal has been fulfilled, you will look back at all of the time you wasted, smothered by fear, anger and senseless worry. The time to be happy is now! The time to enjoy yourself is now! Happiness is not obtaining the pot of gold at the end of the rainbow. Happiness is the journey itself.

Sometimes we get so caught up in the hustle and bustle of trying to make a living that we forget what it's like to live. Sometimes we allow ourselves to become imprisoned by our own personal dramas, to the point that we become blind to all of the good that surrounds us. We must make a conscious effort to take quality time out, to simply have fun and enjoy the process. We must learn to utilize our power of choice and unleash our *humor beings* as a guiding light to lead us through the darkness. When we do this, we might stop concentrating on what we don't have and appreciate what we do have.

If you keep focusing on what you *don't want* or *don't have*, you will be promoting *lack* in your life. When times are tough, that's when you must muster up all of your energy and positive thoughts and focus on what you *do have*.

There is always something to be grateful for. Praise it. Be thankful for it, and you will begin to feel happier. Yes, there is work to be done. Yes, there are deadlines to be met, bills to be paid, and goals to achieve. I know there are problems to be solved, and some of us have a great deal of pain to cope with.

But who says we can't at least try to acquire a healthier attitude and look for the joy in and around our challenges and setbacks?

In all of my years of being a stand-up comedian, I've met many comedians who put their happiness on hold. They couldn't enjoy the process, because they believed they wouldn't be happy until... Over the years I've seen them become transformed into bitter, angry, jealous, and resentful people. It got to the point where some of these comedians didn't even enjoy making people laugh. They allowed themselves to get sucked into the hustle and bustle of the world of show business. Along with that they gave up their right to enjoy the journey.

It was disheartening to see them living such a shallow existence. They would perform from club to club, go from one audition to another, never really enjoying the moment, just waiting and hoping for that big break—for that day when they would finally be happy.

How do you perceive your challenges? Do you perceive them as a curse? Are you someone who asks, "Why me?" Do you feel sorry for yourself and blame situations and other people? Do you feel victimized and cheated? Have you given up and accepted your plight, thinking you can never win?

The fact is, if you believe you can't enjoy yourself at work or at home—you won't. If you insist holding onto the belief that life is unfair—it will be. If you are not happy about anything in your life, I suggest you try changing your perception about it.

Author Marrianne Williamson says that our greatest tool for changing the world is our capacity to change our mind about the world. Your *humor being* can aid you in changing your mind about the world. Remember that your sense of humor is your sense of perspective. It's a choice you have that can help you view the world and all of its problems from a healthier perspective.

As you will see throughout this book, the ability to change your mind to see a stressful and even a tragic situation from a healthier perspective is the ultimate empowerment towards *success and happiness*. This is true because it will eventually determine whether you live your life in tune with love or fear.

High Points to Remember

❧ Things don't always have to go your way or be right before you can be happy.

❧ In order to choose happiness you must understand that you are the creator of your thoughts. When something upsetting happens, it's not the situation that makes you unhappy, it's your thoughts about the situation that cause you to feel a certain way.

❧ Your *humor being* can help you change your thoughts about a particular problem. Viewing any challenge with humor helps feed your brain with positive data, resulting in a happier outcome.

Chapter Four
$\mathcal{H}$umor Reprogramming

A humor reprogramming will help you see,
feel and appreciate the miraculous effects that
humor and laughter can have in your life.

M any people claim to have a wonderful sense of humor, but fail to use it when they need it most. I also believe there are people who simply do not know how to see humor in the midst of challenging times.

If you are one of the many people who find it difficult to see the humor when times get tough, if you are programmed to take life too seriously, might I suggest a *humor reprogramming*? A humor reprogramming will help you see, feel, and appreciate the miraculous effects that humor and laughter can have in your life. A humor reprogramming will show you how to tap into *laughter reservoirs* and how to induce a re-birth of your hidden *humor genes*. Once you are able to unleash these natural powers, you will be well on your way to *becoming a humor being*.

There's a method I use that can help you tap into your laughter reservoir and get your humor genes to work for you. I call this method *pumping your humor muscle*. It's like most things in life worth having...*it takes patience and action*. For example: you can't expect to maintain a healthy and fit body without proper training and discipline. It takes constant conditioning and a great deal of effort to acquire the type of body you desire. You have to eat right and exercise before you start to look and feel healthy.

It's the same thing with trying to condition yourself with humor. When you make an effort every day to try to see the humor in life's absurdities, embarrassing moments, and challenges, you will be pumping and strengthening your humor muscle. And, as with any muscle in your body, the more you pump it, the stronger it gets. In time, you will notice that you have the emotional strength and endurance to take on life's stresses.

THREE STEPS TO PUMP AND STRENGTHEN
YOUR HUMOR MUSCLE.

There are three steps, or exercises, that can help you pump and strengthen your humor muscle.

First, as soon as you wake up, tell yourself it's a great day and that no matter what happens there is a power in you that can overcome any obstacle. Know that you are in control and that you always have a choice. Recite positive affirmations as you get ready to greet the day, like: *"I am in control of my life." "Whatever this day brings, there is something in me that is strong enough to meet it, overcome it, and be blessed by it."*

Second, find something to make you laugh, or at least put a smile on your face before you leave the house for work or wherever it is you have to go. You will be amazed at the power and energy you'll get from doing this every day. In a short time, you will notice that humor ignites creativity, creativity leads to productivity, and productivity can be contagious. Why not start an epidemic of positive energy in and around your life? Why shouldn't you start your day off in a good mood?

Use your imagination. Put your laughter cap on and be observant. It's what I call *observing and developing your humor insights.* It simply means, observe the funny stuff that is around you. Observe your kids. Watch how they grow up to be just like you.

My son thinks he's a comedian. When he was in grade school, he was always making people laugh. But he didn't know when to stop. This started to become a bit of a problem. One day I came home and said, *"How was school today?"*

He looked at me and said, *"Good crowd, good crowd!"*

Trying to hold back my laughter, I said, *"Don't get smart with me."*

57

He looked right at me and said, *"Don't worry, Pop. I don't want to confuse you."*

If you have pets, observe them. They can definitely put a smile on your face. I have come to the conclusion that every cat in the world has a Brooklyn attitude. They walk around like they're Gods gift to the animal kingdom. If cats could talk, they would say, *"Meow. Meow. Ba-da-bing. Meow."*

Have you ever told a cat to go fetch something? It will just sit there and give you a look as if to say, *"Hey, I don't get things. You want something, you tell your best friend Rover to fetch. I'm busy. I've got company comin' over. And when they get here, don't embarrass me with this 'Here Kitty, Kitty' stuff. I got a name! You use it! Even if it is Fluffy, you use it!"*

This is what I'm talking about. It's this type of observation that helps you develop your humor insights. This is how you tap into your *laughter reservoirs* and how you get your *humor genes* circulating. This is the stuff that puts you in a good mood. Hold onto it and take it with you. It's so very simple, and the benefits are priceless.

The third step is to challenge yourself to find the humor in the events that cause you to get upset throughout the day. The purpose of this exercise is to get you to view your challenges and stressful moments as if you were in a movie theatre observing yourself starring in your own hit comedy. Let me explain.

Years ago, I remember viewing the movie *Planes,*

Trains and Automobiles, starring Steve Martin and John Candy. The plot is about two strangers with totally different personalities trying desperately to get home for the Thanksgiving holiday. Due to bad weather, all airline flights are cancelled and the two men are destined to travel together on their long, eventful journey home.

The conflict is that Steve Martin is having a difficult time putting up with John Candy's ways and habits. In one scene, they not only have to share a small hotel room, but they also have to share the same bed. This scene has no dialogue. But just the sight of the two of them laying next to each other gets the audience laughing.

Steve Martin decides to get up and use the bathroom. He notices that John Candy has his clothes hanging all over the place. He proceeds to wash his hands and face. As he's drying off, he shakes his head as if to say, *"What else could go wrong?"* Then he realizes he's drying his face with John Candy's underwear. At this point the entire audience is howling at what is happening on the screen. I noticed I was concentrating more on the audience's response than I was on the movie. I found it very intriguing how people can laugh at a situation that is causing someone else to lose control.

Later on that evening, I asked myself why is it that every time we see a Neil Simon play or view a movie, we become hysterical when the characters experience major conflicts? Basically, the answer is that we are laughing at extensions of ourselves. We are literally laughing off our pain, anger, and fear through the characters in the movie. They represent who we are, what we are, and how ridiculous and difficult we make our lives to be. You wouldn't be able to laugh unless you could relate to what was transpiring on the screen.

Wouldn't it be wonderful if you could view your own emotional outbursts, conflicts, and stressful moments as if they were scenes from your own movie? The benefit in this is that not only are you the star in the movie, but you are also the movie viewer. Allowing yourself to become the movie viewer separates you emotionally from what's happening. When you can separate yourself from what's happening you see it from a different perspective. As a viewer, you are more likely to see the absurdity in the situation. You will more than likely find that you are blowing the entire ordeal out of proportion. Becoming a movie viewer not only enables you to see how ridiculous a particular situation is, but it also allows you to find the humor in it.

Years ago, I was waiting for what I considered to be a very important phone call from my agent. He had left a message the night before stating that three shows that had been booked were now cancelled. Moreover, a television special I was in the running for now looked bleak.

I immediately called him the next morning. His secretary said he was in a meeting. She assured me he would call me as soon as the meeting was over.

Three hours went by, and still no call. I decided to call again. This time his secretary said he was out to lunch. I hung up the phone. I was very angry. All kinds of negative thoughts were going through my head. When thoughts go through my head—negative or positive—I have a tendency to repeat them out loud as I pace back and forth.

A few more hours went by and I had actually convinced myself that my agent didn't care about my needs or my career.

At this point I was overwhelmed by negativity and I started talking to the phone. Now, let me make this clear. I wasn't talking on the phone, I was talking to the phone. *"Let me wait, will you? I don't deserve this kind of treatment! Who do you think you are?!"*

Even my dogs were looking at me as if to say, *"Don't you have to pick it up first?"*

Apparently my wife was observing the entire ordeal. Without missing a beat, she stepped in front of me, grabbed the phone, disconnected the wires from my desk and started yelling at the phone. *"Yeah! Who do you think you are, treating my husband like that? Bad telephone! Bad telephone!"* Then she took it and threw it in the garbage.

I looked at her and said, *"What are you doing?"*

"Honey, I don't know what that phone did to upset you," she said, *"but whatever it was, it will no longer stay in this house."* Then she said, *"Is the fax machine bothering you,*

too? How about the computer? Because if they are, I won't tolerate it!" Then she literally yelled through every room in the house, *"Now hear this! Can I have your attention please? All of the appliances, pieces of furniture and all other inanimate objects! If you do anything to upset my husband, out you go! This is the law! I have spoken!"* Then she quietly walked away.

She burst back into my office, approached the phone that was now in the garbage and said, *"You're not so tough now are you?"* She then turned to me, kissed me on the cheek, patted my head and said, *"You see honey, you just have to learn how to take control."* And walked out of the room.

After watching this crazy woman running around the house, in a rampage, yelling at everything in sight, I noticed that something was different. I was laughing. The question is—Why was I laughing at a situation that only seconds earlier had me emotionally distraught? The answer of course, is that my wife's crazy antics helped me pull myself away from this negative experience. Her comedic ways enabled me to see myself star in a scene from my own comedy movie. As a result, I realized I was blowing the whole thing out of proportion and my emotional state made a complete turn-around. Twenty minutes later, my agent called. I was able to listen to him and tell him my concerns, without the anger and frustrations.

It truly is amazing the power we can acquire when we

allow ourselves the emotional luxury to pull ourselves away from our emotional scenes and give ourselves permission to view them from the audience perspective.

Is this an easy thing to do? Well, for some people it's easier than others. The point is that we all have the power to do this. Whether or not you use this power, is up to you. First, you have to realize what's happening to you. In other words, you must be aware when you are becoming emotionally distraught. Then you must understand what the consequences will be if you stay in that emotional state.

I suggest asking yourself what I call warning questions, i.e., *What will be the consequences if I hold onto the anger? Where is the humor in this? What is the price I will pay if I don't laugh this off?* These types of questions act like radar, warning you that you are entering a negative energy field. More importantly, warning questions are constant reminders that there are better ways to deal with the frustrating and chaotic events that turn up in our lives.

The challenge with a *humor reprogramming*, as with any other self-help reprogramming is that it requires time, change, patience, and commitment. The question I am most often asked is, *"How can I find humor in a situation that has me so upset?"* I can understand the concern here. In fact, trying to laugh when you're angry almost sounds like a contradiction. The point here, however, is that you're not so much laughing because you're angry. You're laughing because of the repercussions of how the anger will eventually affect you if you don't do something about it. You're using humor as a healthier alternative.

Quite simply the answer is practice. That's what a *humor reprogramming* is all about. Practice. Remember, it takes conditioning in order to see the humor in an upsetting situation. You have to make a daily effort to pump and strengthen your humor muscle. I know this sounds repetitious, but I will continue to make this point in different ways throughout this book. I can't express this enough. *The more you try to rejuvenate your humor genes, the more they become a part of who you are.*

One reason we find it difficult to find humor in the midst of hard times is that we were brought up to take life too seriously. How many times have you heard this when you were growing up?

> *Will you stop laughing!?*
>
> *Wipe that smirk off your face!*
>
> *That's not funny! Why are you laughing?*
>
> *Will you please grow up?*
>
> *Why can't you be serious?*
>
> *Everything to you is a big joke!!*

It's no wonder we can't see the humor when life gets tough—we've smothered our humor and laughter genes. God forbid you should find some humor in the middle of a crisis or while trying to solve a problem. Listen to what we say to ourselves while trying to solve a difficult problem at work. *"It's time to take the bull by the horns."* I don't think so! You take the bull by the horns, Mr. Macho! I'll be outside the corral laughing my butt off! And while you're exhausted and licking your wounds from trying to wrestle that bull, I'll be energized and ready to solve the problem.

I went to therapy for about a year, read dozens of self-help books, listened to motivational tapes and attended quite a few seminars. Still my life wasn't working. Why? Well, first of all, I was too serious. I had a lot of anger to deal with. I had fears and self-doubt to confront. These things were ruining my life and I couldn't find anything funny about that. At least that's what I thought at the time. I believed I had to grab the bull by the horns. There was no time for mistakes or setbacks. And, there was no reason for laughter.

Secondly, I never fully understood that the therapist, books, tapes, and seminars were just the tools, not the answers. I never fully realized that my responsibility was to learn how to use the tools so I could reprogram and build the life I wanted. To make that possible I had to implement the most important tool of all: My sense of humor. I simply had to lighten up. Humor not only helped me build a new life, but it also helped knock down the one I was previously living in.

Let me make this perfectly clear. My life didn't change

overnight. It took years before I noticed any major changes. As with any kind of reprogramming, you must realize that you are going to have setbacks and disappointments. There will be times when you'll think that your life is getting worse instead of better. It's OK, keep reminding yourself that you're attempting to live your life a totally different way than you're used to. You have been conditioned to cling to old habits from the past. The key is to recognize when your *humor being* is working. In other words, make a mental note, or better yet write down in a journal, how your ability to see the humor in a stressful situation helped you feel better. Note how it elevated your energy level or how it made a difference in a decision you made. Be aware of outcomes and consequences.

By doing this you are reinforcing that it's working! Then the next time you are confronted with a challenging situation your thought process will automatically remind you what worked before. That's an opportunity for you to use the same type of humor on something similar again.

It's also important to take special notice when family members, friends, and co-workers comment on how much more at ease you are or how your attitude has changed for the better. Eventually, your *humor being* will become a part of who you are.

HIGH POINTS TO REMEMBER

⊱ As soon as you wake up tell yourself it's a great day and that no matter what happens, there is a power in you that can overcome any adversity.

⊱ Find something to make you laugh or at least to put a smile on your face before you leave the house. Put your laughter cap on and be observant. It's called observing and developing your humor insights.

⊱ Find the humor in the events that cause you to get upset. View your challenges and stressful moments as if you were viewing yourself starring in your own hit comedy. As a movie viewer you are more likely to see the absurdity in the situation.

Chapter Five

It's a Matter of Choice

*Sometimes a second is all the hope you need
before you decide to give up. Humor gives
you that second because it nips negative
thoughts in the bud, before they blossom into
emotional havoc.*

Choice! *The key is choice. You have
options. You need not spend your life wallowing in failure, ignorance, grief, poverty, shame, and self-pity. But
hold on! If this is true, then why have so many among us
apparently elected to live in that manner?*

*The answer is obvious. Those who live in unhappy
failure have never exercised their options for a better way
of life because they have never been aware that they had
any choices.*

The above words by Og Mandino in his book *The
Choice* state very simply how our inability to utilize our

power of choice can affect our entire lives. Life is about choices. Every situation is a choice. We choose how to react to situations. We choose how people will affect our mood. We choose to be in a good mood or a bad mood. The bottom line: It's the choices we make that determine how we live our lives. Once you can say to yourself that you have a choice on how to deal with a problem or a crisis, you are sending a message to your brain that you are in control of the situation, instead of the situation controlling you. You are not at the mercy of the situation.

You can choose to believe you are helpless and at the mercy of life's unpleasant twists of fate and misfortunes. You can choose to believe some people are lucky and some are destined to a life of misery and despair. If this is what you believe, then that will be your reality.

On the other hand, you could choose to believe you have a choice in your affairs, that you are not helpless, that you are responsible for your actions, and that somehow, somewhere along the way you create, direct, or influence your success and happiness.

In his book, *Man's Search For Meaning*, Viktor Frankl shares what he learned from his experiences as a prisoner in Auschwitz during World War II.

Everything can be taken from a man but one thing, the last of the human freedoms—to choose one's attitude in any set of circumstances, to choose one's own way.

If we could comprehend the meaning and power behind these words, we could set ourselves free from much of the pain, fear, and uncertainty we experience throughout our lives. In essence, what Viktor Frankl is telling us is the axiom, *"You may not be able to control what happens to you, but you can always choose and control how you think about what happens."* I would like to add that you can also choose your attitude and the actions you take when something does happen. This should be a preamble before trying to solve any problem, big or small.

This is where a sense of humor can help tremendously. Our sense of humor is our sense of perspective. It's a choice we all have on how to deal with life's uncertainties and tough times. When we don't take advantage of such choices we feel victimized or cheated.

Surrounded by total devastation and horror, Viktor Frankl knew he had a choice; and at times he chose to utilize the healing power of humor to help ease his pain. He talks about how he trained a friend of his to develop a sense of humor. They promised to tell each other at least one amusing story each day about some incident that would happen after they were liberated. A kind of cabaret was even improvised by some of the prisoners from time to time. There were songs, poems, jokes, and underlying satire. It was effective and it helped them forget. Most of the prisoners would attend, in spite of their fatigue and the fact they would miss their daily portions of food by going.

"Humor was another of the soul's weapons in the fight for self-preservation. It is well-known that humor, more than anything else in the human make-up, can afford an aloofness and an ability to rise above any situation, even if only for a few seconds."

Sometimes a second is all the hope you need before you decide to give up. Humor gives you that second because it nips negative thoughts in the bud before they blossom into emotional havoc. Emotional havoc is a series of negative thoughts that eventually lead to the deterioration of the self. When the self deteriorates, you feel as if every ounce of energy has been drained from your body.

Viktor Frankl's use of humor was an intuitive calling from his higher self. It was his *humor being* coming to his aid. It was his choice to heed the calling that helped him survive one of the greatest calamities of all time. Even if only for moments at a time, humor gave him and others the hope to rise above the horrors of Auschwitz.

A BLESSING IN DISGUISE

The biggest inspiration in my life is my brother Michael. No one has taught me more about how to embrace the changes in life and how to enjoy the process than he has. He is 100 percent disabled as a result of the Vietnam War. Twenty-one feet of his small intestine were either blown out on the battlefield or removed on the operating table, leaving him with only one foot to live on. His bowels were wired until they healed, and a portion of his large intestine was removed as well. His medical records were sent to various experts throughout the world. The diagnosis always came back with the same grim response: *"It seemed highly unlikely, if not impossible, for anyone to survive that kind of wound."*

I remember the first time I saw Michael in St. Alban's Naval Hospital in Queens, New York. If my parents had not been by his side when I walked into the room, I would not have known it was my brother lying there. He had gone from 175 pounds to 85 pounds. It took every ounce of energy for me to control my emotions. He was heavily sedated and going in and out of consciousness.

Throughout the day, I kept hoping that a doctor would come in and say, *"Don't worry. Everything will be okay. He will be up and on his feet in no time."* But that did not happen. In fact, the opposite happened. A doctor came in, but not with the message I was hoping for. He approached my parents, and said the words we all dreaded to hear, *"I'm sorry, but it doesn't look like he is going to make it. It would be a miracle for him or anyone to survive such an ordeal."*

For a moment there was silence in the room, followed by tears and painful moans. Two of my brother's friends from high school, who were in the room, went over to embrace my mom and dad. His Marine Corps buddy was hitting the wall saying, *"Why?"*

As all of this was going on I remembered staring at my

brother, wondering if this were the last time I would ever see him. Then I noticed Michael's hand slowly rising from his side. He must have been aware of what was going on. He must have heard the doctor's diagnosis, because he clenched his fist, and to my surprise, I noticed his middle finger starting to protrude straight out from all the rest!

Although the person I was looking at did not look like my brother, I knew then, from the raising of that middle finger, that the spirit that constituted Michael John Rizzo was still alive and strong. I knew then that somehow, some way, Michael was going to make it. He still had his *sense of humor*! He still had his wits about him! That extended finger was his salute to recovery. It was his opinion of the doctor's diagnosis. And to be quite honest, the raising of that middle finger was the answer he gave to everything they said he could not or would not be able to do.

First, they said that he would not live for very long. Obviously they were wrong. They also said that he would probably have to eat cereal, fruit and baby food for the rest of his life. He did have a difficult time eating food with any substance. After all, we are talking about someone with only one foot of his small intestine. As soon as Michael swallowed anything, it was ready to come out.

Yes, it was discouraging, to say the least, but my brother insisted he was going to eat whatever he wanted, whenever he wanted. As he said to one of the doctors,

"Don't tell me what I can eat and what I can't eat. I'm going to eat a bowl of pasta, even if I have to sit on the toilet while I eat it!"

It was this attitude that enabled Michael to adapt to and take control of his new digestive system. Doctors still don't know how he does it, but he eats anything he wants to and enjoys it. He is the only man in medical history to survive this kind of wound. In fact, he is doing more than just surviving—he is living. He's married, has two children, and he is the principal of a junior high school. His activities include golf and whitewater rafting. He has more energy and enthusiasm than anyone I know. If you were to see him today, you would not know he was wounded.

Some say it was a miracle. I believe we all have opportunities to perform our own miracles. It is a matter of what we choose to believe and what thoughts we allow ourselves to concentrate on from day to day. Many of the wounded in that hospital gave up. They allowed themselves to feel victimized and cheated. They allowed fear to take control, eventually leading them to lives filled with anger, resentment, and hopelessness. I'm not making any judgments. I'm sure they had valid reasons for feeling the way they did. But it was the perception of their challenges—what they concentrated on—that led them to their world of hopelessness and despair.

My brother, on the other hand, had a unique way of

perceiving his challenge. He formulated a belief system that enabled him to search for a brighter alternative. He looked for the open window when the door was slammed in his face. He never asked, *"Why me?"* Instead, he said to the world, *"This is me, and I'm going to make it!"* He never concentrated on what was missing from his life. He just took what he had left and went far and beyond what anyone thought he could. Even though he was in tremendous pain, he never blamed the war, the Marine Corps or his country. He took full responsibility for his actions.

Every day that went by, doctors became more amazed at the rate he was progressing. Michael was in the hospital for over a year. He literally defied the odds that were set against him. Helping him defy those odds was the utilization of his *humor being*. It shielded him from anguish and pain. Every time a specialist told him he would not be able to do something, up went the middle finger, followed by some sarcastic remark or sick joke.

One day he was being reprimanded by a doctor for eating a sandwich. My brother looked at the doctor and said, *"The difference between you and me, Doc, is that you keep concentrating on the 21 feet of intestine I no longer have. And I keep concentrating on the one foot I do have."* Then Michael belched and said, *"Now, what's for dessert?"*

This type of attitude strengthened his conviction that he was going to do whatever they told him he could not do. I swear there were times when he seemed to love the challenge. He found great joy in proving them wrong. Every diagnosis he foiled put another notch on his victory belt and another step towards getting well.

Michael's ability to laugh enabled him to open up and receive the love that was being sent by family and friends. Being open to receive love is what made it possible for him to give love back. It was this total acceptance of love that gave him the hope he needed to create miracles in his life.

His enjoyment for life was, and still is, extraordinary. Another key toward overcoming his challenge was that Michael never put his happiness on hold. Others said, *"I'll enjoy myself when I get better,"* or *"How can I enjoy myself in this condition?"* My brother took a different stance and said, *"I'll try to enjoy myself now."* As a result, he gradually got better. He seemed to sense the importance of moving forward, not looking back, and enjoying the moment.

When Michael was released from the hospital he weighed 95 pounds. He decided to go to college. Some people were a bit apprehensive about this decision. They did not know if he would be able to do it in his condition. Plus, he had not been Mr. Whiz kid in high school—to say the least. We're talking about a guy who was kept back three times in high school, and had no academic or vocational skills at all. My mom and dad were concerned that his lack of education and physical disability would prove to be too much for him. Again, he amazed all of us. He graduated from college with degrees in history, education, and administration. And, I might add, he is a bit of a financial whiz, too.

I tell this story because it is not what happens to us that determines whether we are happy or successful. It's the choices we make. It's how we perceive and what we do about what happens that makes the difference. Some people seem to have every advantage within their reach, and still they manage to destroy their lives and sabotage their success. Then there are those who seem to have every disadvantage thrown their way, yet they take what appears to be the greatest of tragedies and somehow make their lives work. My brother's sense of humor helped him form a set of beliefs and values that continue to direct his life from a sense of advantage rather than a disadvantage. He took every challenge and turned it into an opportunity.

When Michael was in the hospital, sickness and death surrounded him. He was in a room filled with young men with parts of their bodies missing. They were in pain physically and mentally. He witnessed bodies brought in and out for over a year. He heard their cries. He felt their pain. Through all of this, plus having to deal with his own pain, he insisted on focusing all of his energy on what would need to be done to get out of there, and what he was going to do once he did.

My brother has admitted to me on a few occasions that he probably would not be as successful as he is today, if it had not been for the major change that took place in his life. He views the challenge as a blessing in disguise. He used it as a tool to move forward. This is not to say he is glad that he was wounded—rather, that he chose to do something about it when it did happen.

Sometimes you need to view how you want your life to be on the TV screen in your mind. Of course, as with any television, you are in control of the volume and you have a choice as to what program to watch. If, for example, you are viewing a program that is loud, offensive, and filled with negativity and bringing you down—you have a choice. You can choose to continue watching the program or you can choose to change the channel to a program that will make you feel alive, happy and positive.

That is exactly what my brother did. He would only watch the programs that showed how he wanted his life to be. Every now and then, because of negative static from his surroundings, the channels would automatically change to negative programming—the Misery Channel, the Hopeless Channel, the Despair and the Pain Channel. These channels are not conducive to promoting a happy and successful life.

My brother, however, knew he was in control of the remote. And quite often it was his *humor being*—his ability to laugh—that gave him that control. He would immediately change the channel to a program that would make him feel strong and confident. He tuned into the Hope

Channel, the Faith and Love Channels, the Comedy and Laughter Channels.

In order to be truly successful and happy, you must focus on what will make your life work for you. You must come to an understanding that you have a choice as to what channels to view on the television screen in your mind. You must believe you are in control of the remote.

And finally, you must be aware that what you choose will determine the quality of success, happiness, and inner peace you will enjoy.

High Points to Remember

&> Once you say to yourself that you have a choice on how to deal with a problem, you are in control of the situation instead of the situation controlling you.

&> Your sense of humor is your sense of perspective. It's a choice you have on how to deal with uncertainties and tough times. It's when you don't take advantage of such choices that you feel victimized or cheated.

&> You can perform miracles in your life. It's a matter of what you choose to believe and what thoughts you concentrate on from day to day.

Chapter *Six*

The Power of Laughter

It was always the spirit of love that pulled us through. And it was the power of laughter that kept us from falling apart.

We live in a world that moves very fast. Many people get lost in the shuffle. On top of our personal problems and everyday pressures, we read the newspaper and listen to the news to learn that corporations are being forced to downsize and massive technological advancements in the workplace are forcing people to change their lives. Crime, disease, prejudice, and violence are running rampant. The divorce rate is at an all-time high and war seems to be the only answer to solve differences between nations. We need something to reduce this tension—this fast pace that life throws at us every day. I honestly believe one of those things is our ability to simply laugh it off.

People go to comedy clubs because they want to laugh. Why do they want to laugh? Because laughter makes them feel good! That's the bottom line. Laughter simply makes you feel good. Even if you're having a bad day, when you laugh, life doesn't seem so bad after all. In fact, your life seems to go up a few notches on the happiness scale.

When people laugh their bodies give off a special hormone called endorphins. Endorphins are natural painkillers that alleviate pain due to stress. So throw away the Valium, aspirin, drugs and alcohol. Laugh it off and live longer!

Humor and laughter are wonderful, easily accessible tools for bringing comfort and health into our lives. Norman Cousins claims to have cured himself of cancer through positive thinking and the power of laughter. He watched hours of film clips every day of *Laurel and Hardy*, *Abbot and Costello*, the *Three Stooges*, and anything he could find to make him laugh. He literally laughed his way to good health.

Mother Teresa, who constantly worked among the hungry, despaired, and dying, insisted that her hospital wards be filled with laughter. She believed that laughter was one of the strongest forces towards health, productivity, strength and spirituality.

Do you know what the sad truth is? The same people

who are at the comedy clubs laughing hysterically return home, and in a short time get into the same rut they were in before. They don't realize they have the power within themselves to laugh off their own absurdities and hard times. They forfeit their right to choose, and thereby allow fear to control their lives.

Let me make this perfectly clear. You don't need me to make you laugh. You don't need a comedian to help you laugh off your fears. It helps, it's fun, and it's great therapy, but you don't have to depend on other people to make you feel good.

Each and every one of you has what it takes to laugh off your fears and stressful moments. I know, it takes a certain amount of courage to laugh in the midst of all the chaos and problems in our world. But sometimes laughter seems to be the only sane cure for all of the insanity that surrounds us.

Laughter puts people in good moods. Good moods enhance one's ability to think clearly, thus making it easier to find solutions to problems, says Daniel Goleman. In his book *Emotional Intelligence*, Dr. Goleman says that one way to help someone think through a problem is to tell them a joke. Laughing, like elation, seems to help people think more broadly and associate more freely; which is important in recognizing complex relationships and situations, and foreseeing the consequences of a decision.

LAUGH OFF THE FEAR

A few years ago my mom was notified by a group of doctors that the right artery from her brain to her heart was clogged. She had to undergo major surgery. A week before the surgery, the family met with a specialist. The purpose of the meeting was to review hospital procedures and to answer any questions we had regarding the operation.

When the doctor walked into his office, he stopped in mid-stride when he saw the crowd that was waiting for him. Apparently he only anticipated my mom and dad, not the entire Rizzo family (my wife and me, my two brothers and their wives, my sister and her husband, and of course, mom and dad). Believe me, the Brady bunch we are not! I have a brother named Rocky. Rocky Rizzo. Need I say more?

I suppose having all of us in one small room only added tension to an already stressful situation. From the doctor's perspective it probably felt like an interrogation rather than a consultation. After we introduced ourselves the doctor proceeded to ask my mom some questions. *"Do you have any problems hearing?"* he asked.

Mom has a wonderful sense of humor, and decided this was a good time to take advantage of it. *"What?"* she replied.

We all started giggling. But the doctor did not get it. He repeated the question, only more loudly. *"DO YOU HAVE ANY PROBLEMS HEARING?"*

85

"NO! AND WHY ARE YOU YELLING?" Mom replies.

At that point, we all broke out laughing. The doctor said, *"Oh, I get it. You're a comedian."*

Pointing at me, Mom says, *"No, he's the comedian. If you can't tell the difference, I'm out of here!"*

The doctor sat back in his chair, shook his head, laughed and said, *"Oh, it's gonna be one of those days."*

"Stop whining!" Mom says. *"I'm the one who needs surgery!"*

I remember thinking, *"Oh my God, she's on a roll!"*

The doctor continued asking questions. *"Do you have a problem with losing your memory at all?"*

Mom thought about it and said, *"No."* Then she leaned towards the doctor and whispered, *"But can you tell me who all these people are and why I am here?"*

My mom's sense of humor and her ability to make us laugh put all of us at ease, including the doctor. As a result we were able to break down that wall of fear and ask important questions regarding the surgical procedure. Everyone walked out of the office feeling uplifted and confident that surgery was the right option. But more importantly, we believed Mom was in the hands of a very qualified surgeon and in the hands of people who cared.

As I recall, we kept our wits about us, even on the day of the surgery. Mom was in a waiting room with six other patients. My brothers and I were cracking jokes about hospital procedures. We had everyone, including the hospital staff, laughing hysterically.

I must admit the highlight was when I took a rubber surgical glove from a bin and blew it up like a balloon. Once the five fingers were inflated I went down on all fours, put the balloon under my stomach, and did my impersonation of a cow. I don't know what possessed me, but I took everyone by surprise when I approached the head nurse and asked her where I should go for an Utter-O-Gram.

I don't know why this was funny. I guess some things strike people in different ways. The lady in the bed next to my mom was laughing hard and screaming for a bedpan at the same time. (I'm proud to say that the bedpan didn't make it there in time!) It was then that the nurse, who was trying to be stern with me but couldn't stop laughing, escorted me to my chair and said, *"If you can't behave, you will leave me with no choice but to send you to the psychiatric ward!"*

"Sorry, Nurse Ratched," I replied in my best Jack Nicholson voice. *"I'll be good. Please don't send me to the cuckoo's nest!"* I thought everyone was going to die from laughing—before they even made it to the operating table.

Mom still had her wits about her, even after she was sedated and they were wheeling her off to surgery. I remember I leaned over the bed, with tears in my eyes and I said, *"Mom, I love you."*

She slowly opened her eyes and said, *"Forget it, son. You're not getting my Bud Lite!"*

We waited at the hospital for over six hours before we were told that the operation had been successful. During much of that time I traveled into my past. It was as if someone had captured my entire life on film and played it on fast forward for me to review.

I saw good times, filled with joy and happiness; and I saw many difficult times, filled with pain, sadness and heartache. Yes, my family, like many other families, has had its share of life's unexpected twists and turns. But somehow we always managed to pull through—in spite of the scars some of us still have.

I remember asking myself, *"How were we able to survive so many of life's calamities? How were we able to deal with so much pain?"*

No sooner had I asked myself these questions then I looked over at my sister and saw her arms around my father. The answer was very clear—LOVE! It was always the spirit of love that pulled us through. And it was the power of laughter that kept us from falling apart. It was the unleashing of our *humor beings* that always kept us connected to the spirit of love, and that connection prevails today.

TAKE CONTROL

Let me give you an example of how important it is to be in control of your emotions and how the simple ability to laugh can help you maintain control.

Years ago I was in New York City, driving a rental car that kept breaking down. It was 98 degrees, the air conditioning didn't work, and sweat was pouring from my body. To make matters worse, I was in the world's biggest traffic jam and I was already 45 minutes late for a very important audition.

I started to feel this snowball of negative emotions building up. I said to myself out loud, *"What else could possibly go wrong?"* I soon realized that was the wrong question to ask. Whenever you ask a question like that the universe has its own way of answering you.

I drove up to the toll booth with beads of sweat running down my face. I tried really hard to control my emotions. I reached into my pocket to pay the toll—and realized I had left my money at home. I sat there in total amazement at the series of events that were keeping me from my destination.

I started to take it personally. I actually believed that life was out to get me that day—and it was succeeding.

For a moment I was in a daze. I was unaware of the cars beeping and people cursing at me. The guy in the toll booth finally asked (sarcastically), *"Can I help you?"*

I don't know what possessed me to say this, but my reply was, *"Yeah. I'll have a couple of burgers, two fries and a Coke. And get something for yourself there, Sparky!"*

He looked at me, as only a New Yorker can, and said, *"We don't have food here!"*

"Well," I replied nervously, *"then you better get some because you're holding up traffic!"* As I said this I noticed he was starting to laugh. Much to my surprise, so was I.

The long line of drivers behind me, however, did not join in the laughter. There were horns honking and people cursing, *"Come on, we gotta get moving!"* *"What the hell is the problem up there?"* Then, my newfound friend stuck his head out from the toll booth, motioned to the line of cars, and said, *"Sorry, we ran out of food. Try the next booth!"*

By then we were hysterical over the absurdity of the situation. We were high-fiving each other—and the coolest thing is that he let me go without paying. He said, *"This toll is on me, buddy. Thanks. I really needed to laugh today!"*

I looked at him and said, *"Believe me, so did I!"* We shook hands, wished each other a great day, and I drove away from that toll booth in a totally different mood.

As a result, I was able to plant positive thoughts in my head and think of constructive ways to deal with the important audition I had coming up. Guess what? I had a great audition! It's a good thing I did, because it led to the most important break in my career. That's how I got my ShowTime television special, which paved the way to many other opportunities.

Think about this. What would have happened if I had gone to the audition in the mood that I was in before the toll booth incident? I wouldn't have had a chance.

Believe me, I tried everything to control the situation. After all, I read all of the books on positive thinking and positive affirmations. I thought I was an expert. I found out that day that positive thinking and reciting positive affirmations doesn't always work; because there are times when you are in such an overwhelmingly negative emotional state that your brain isn't going to buy the fact that everything is okay.

I mean, there I was, sitting behind the wheel of a stalling car without air conditioning, sweating in 98 degrees, stuck in the world's biggest traffic jam, and late for my audition—reciting affirmations out loud over and over. *"Everything is going as planned. I am in control of this situation. I am the radiating center of love and peace."* Just then someone beeped their horn. I motioned to him with my fist and shouted, *"Pick a number, pal!"* Not only was I frustrated and angry because of my ordeal; I also felt totally inadequate—because I couldn't think positively and get control of my emotions.

When I started to laugh, however, I was able to think positively and visualize how I wanted my audition to go.

Do you know why? When you start laughing at a stressful or highly emotional situation your brain is no longer concentrating on that negative thought. In fact, your brain is now somewhere else laughing at something ridiculous that you just did. Even if your brain goes back to the negative thought, it won't be as overpowering as it was before, because you have stopped the snowball effect. You have calmed down your nervous system to the point where you can think positively and take control. That's what I did. I took control.

That's the first time in my life I realized how important it was to be in control of my emotions, and how laughter helped me take control.

You never know when opportunity is going to knock, and when it does, you have to be prepared. I can't tell you how many opportunities I've blown in my life because I couldn't control my emotions. I can't tell you how many bridges I burned because I made decisions when I was in an unhealthy state of mind.

It doesn't matter what you call it. You can call it karma, payback, or the laws of cause and effect. It doesn't matter. The fact is, the choices you make will determine the actions you take. The actions you take will determine who you are and where you go. This holds true on any level of your life, in all your personal and professional relationships.

LAUGHTER = LEARNING

There are people who believe that if someone is having too much fun at work, they're simply not doing the job properly. Whenever I speak to groups, I always stress the importance of making sure that everyone in the organization knows they have the freedom to laugh and to enjoy the process. *"Intellectual benefits of a good laugh,"* says author Daniel Goleman, *"are most striking when it comes to solving a problem that demands a creative solution."*

One study found that people who had just watched a video of television bloopers were better at solving a puzzle long-used by psychologists to test creative thinking. In the test people are given a candle, matches, and a box of tacks. They are asked to attach the candle to a corkboard wall so it will burn without dripping wax on the floor.

"Given this challenge, most people fall into 'functional fixedness'," says Goleman. *"They think about using the objects in the most conventional ways. But, people who have just watched a funny film, compared to people who have watched a film about math or who have exercised, were more likely to see an alternative use for the box holding the tacks. They came up with the creative solution of tacking the box to the wall and using it as a candleholder."*

A study done at San Diego State University followed students who attended a series of lectures that contained wit, laughter, and anecdotes. These students achieved higher test scores than students who attended the same lectures without the humor. *"When the mouth is open for laughter,"* wrote Dr. Virginia Tooper, *"you may be able to shove in a little food for thought."*

I realized how powerful laughter could be when I taught eighth-grade English on Long Island, New York. Believe me, you needed a sense of humor and a gun— and not necessarily in that order! I knew that the attention span of my best student was about 20 minutes out of a 45 minute class. Quite often I reverted to humor to get my students back into the lesson plan. There was one class in particular that I remember. We were going over the soliloquies of Shakespeare, and my students just weren't paying attention. Without missing a beat, I immediately went into Sylvester Stallone as Hamlet. *"Ahh to be, or ahh ... not to be. Ahh ... that is ahh the question ... Or ahh is it the answer? Anyway, whether it is nobler in the minds of ahh ... ohh, ahh I'd like to buy a vowel. Yeah, the letter Yo."*

I immediately got their attention and they returned to the lesson plan. What else could I have done to get their attention? I could have slammed my book down on the desk and yelled, *"You people better pay attention, because if you don't, you are going to fail the test! Now, I want everyone's eyes focused on me right now!"* I might have had their eyes looking at me, but would they have been paying attention? I doubt it. My ability to make them laugh helped me enjoy my job and helped them enjoy the process—which I believe helped them learn more.

When learning is fun everyone benefits. This holds true in every aspect of our lives. No matter who you are or what you do; whether you are on the learning end or the teaching end, if you are enjoying the process, you are simply going to do it better.

Why do you think *Sesame Street* has been so success-ful all these years? Children from all over the world watch this show. They sit in front of the TV and watch all of these crazy characters, with their crazy antics and funny voices. The children are having so much fun you couldn't drag them away. On another level, they are ingesting a tremen-dous amount of learning material and knowledge. Why? Because they are laughing as they learn!

HIGH POINTS TO REMEMBER

⁊& Laughter can put you in a good mood. Good moods enhance your ability to think clearly, thus making it easier to find solutions to problems.

⁊& When you laugh your body gives off a special hormone called an endorphin. Endorphins are natural painkillers that eliminate pain due to stress.

⁊& When you start laughing at a stressful situation your brain is no longer concentrating on negative thoughts. Your brain is now somewhere else, laughing at something ridiculous you just did. This calms your nervous system so you can think positively and take control.

Chapter Seven

Humor in the Workplace

Whenever you are dealing with someone who is difficult, it's never a matter of who's right or who's wrong. It's about advantages and disadvantages.

Whenever I speak to groups about maintaining a healthy attitude in the workplace, I stress the importance of coming from a foundation of emotional stability. I inform them that there is one thing the people who they are doing business with want more than anything else, and that is to *feel good about themselves.* Everything else revolves around that. The sale, whether they recommend you to someone else, and all decisions concerning repeat business are based on them feeling good about themselves.

Yes, the price and quality of what you offer is important. So is your knowledge and expertise. But you won't

97

even make it to first base if they detect that you have a negative or uncaring attitude.

In general, this holds true in all relationships. We want to feel good about ourselves. We are more at peace with ourselves and happier in our surroundings when we are with people who have positive attitudes. We want to associate ourselves with people who make us laugh and who are fun to be with. It's easier to trust and to confide in people who make us feel good. We tend to put up a wall or try to avoid people who are negative, rude and pushy or always complaining.

The people who you associate with on a professional level will have a difficult time feeling good about themselves if they sense you are not feeling good about yourself. If they sense that you have a bad attitude or feel that you don't care, you create unhealthy feelings. This can result in them taking their business somewhere else.

So, if your day isn't going as planned, stop. Know that you have a choice. If the workload is becoming overload, stop. Know that you have a choice. If someone who is irate confronts you, stop. Know you have a choice. Know that you always have a choice. Then choose the way that will ground you to a foundation of emotional stability.

Successful people know that they are going to have their share of tough times and setbacks in the workplace. They also know that they have a choice on how to deal with them. You can be an expert in your chosen field. You can have degrees from the finest schools with the highest honors. You can know everything there is to know about your organization, but it won't mean anything unless you have the emotional stability to deal with the unexpected. Knowledge by itself is only that—knowledge. Knowledge combined with emotional stability, however, leads to wisdom. It is the wise person who succeeds on all levels of life.

The key is to know that no matter what happens, there is a power within you that can lift you up and raise you above any obstacle. Your *humor being* can play a major role in unleashing this power. Laughter, in particular, can help release the fuel to start this power in motion.

If you watched the hit television show *M.A.S.H.* you witnessed how effective humor can be at work. The character called Hawkeye, played by Alan Alda, had his *humor being* working overtime.

His *humor being* was his shield of armor against the perils of war. As with everyone else in the M.A.S.H. unit, Hawkeye's responsibility was to save lives. But they had to do it against incredible odds. Most of the time they had to operate on very little sleep, few supplies, poor lighting, and quite often while under fire. Through all of the pain, blood and anguish you could always count on Hawkeye to counterattack with his sense of humor.

His *humor being* was his greatest assistant in helping

him save lives. His rapid-fire sarcastic wit gave him the courage and the emotional stability to keep moving in spite of the misery. Hawkeye knew intuitively that his *humor being* was the only savior in a place where there seemed to be such little hope.

ANECDOTAL MIMICRY

Many times throughout your professional and personal lives you will encounter stressful situations. A common situation is how to deal with irrational and rude people who throw their authority around as if the world revolved around their needs. If you are not careful, you could leave yourself wide open for emotional attack and allow the other person's unhealthy attitude to affect your emotional well being. This can cause you to respond on that person's level and perhaps take actions that will more than likely lead to undesirable results. This, in turn, could also leave you emotionally unbalanced for the entire day, affecting every decision you make.

Years ago I was giving a seminar on the importance of maintaining a healthy state of mind to a large group of Residence Inn sales and customer relations people. I noticed a woman who was frantically raising, or should I say flapping, both of her arms to get my attention. I figured I better ask her what she wanted before she flew out of her seat.

She jumped up, and in a defying tone, said, *"I under-*

stand the importance of being in control of your emotions and maintaining a healthy state of mind. But I work behind the front desk at Residence Inn, and you tell me how I'm supposed to maintain a healthy state of mind when I have a rude, sarcastic and loud customer practically in my face! No matter what I try to do to help, it's not good enough! They stand there, with their arrogant attitude, and try to belittle me in front of everyone else! You tell me what I'm supposed to do!"

"By the excitement in your voice," I said, "this must have happened recently."

"Yes," she said, "a few days ago. And it still bothers me."

Many of the other participants acknowledged the woman's comments. And some shared their own experiences in dealing with irate people. It was surprising for me to discover that a few of them were actually reliving the unpleasant situation and still holding onto the anger, as if it had just happened.

I told them I understood how a rude and irate customer could cause them to become emotionally upset. But, I also explained that when someone verbally attacks you with insults and demands, it's not the irate person who causes you to become emotionally distraught. It's your thoughts about that person and what's being said that causes you to become upset. You are allowing that person or situation to get to you.

Furthermore, when you say that a person or a situation has caused you to become upset, this indicates you have given your personal power away. You have actually given another person or a situation permission to do what they want with your emotions. You have surrendered to their ways. You have given up your power to choose a better way.

And you have proven to yourself and to everyone else that you are not in control of your life.

I suggested that one very effective way to keep power and to stay in control of a provoking or threatening situation was to turn your *humor being* loose. I then addressed the woman who asked the question. I explained to her that I was going to answer her question by doing a little role-playing. I would be both the irate customer and the front desk person.

I also explained that what the group was about to witness might seem childish and out of the ordinary—but if they used this method with anyone who was irate or demanding it would work 100 percent of the time. I then proceeded with my little skit.

The front desk person is in her office. She hears the pounding of the bell on the front desk. Ding, ding. Ding, ding, ding! Ding, ding, ding! Ding, ding!

Front Desk Person: Yes sir. Can I help you?

Irate Customer: Yes, you can help me! I just went to my room, and guess what? There's no fireplace! I made this reservation two months ago! I'm tired. I want a room with a fireplace and I want it now!

Front Desk Person: Well, sir. I'll check.

Irate Customer: Excuse me! There is nothing to check! Just go into your little computer and get me a room with a fireplace—and get it now! It's bad enough I had to wait two hours for the damn room to be ready! Then, when I get there, there's no fireplace! What kind of dump is this, anyway?

After this dialogue I asked the group what they would do when confronted with a situation like this. They all shrugged their shoulders, expect for one fellow who yelled out, *"That's easy. I'm from New York. Shoot 'em!"*

I turned to the woman who asked the question. *"How would you handle this situation?"*

"I don't know," she said, *"but that's exactly what I'm talking about."*

I suggested that in a situation like this, she should immediately put a smile on her face and assure the customer she was going to do everything in her power to rectify the problem. Then she should excuse herself, go into her office, close the door, and take a deep breath. Once there, she should picture in her mind what had just transpired. But, I suggested, she should ask her *humor being* for guidance, and let loose and mimic the entire situation.

I emphasized she should go crazy with this. She should use her imagination and repeat and exaggerate the same words he said to her. She should change the pitch in her voice and animate, amplify, and repeat the entire ordeal as if they were in some kind of comedy or cartoon on fast-forward, i.e.:

Front Desk Person: (*Mimicking and dancing around the room*)

I want a fireplace-in-my-room! I made this reservation two months ago! I waited two hours for this room!

Well excuse me, your Majesty! But I don't have any more rooms with a fireplace! (faster) But I'll tell you what I'll do. If you will just wait right here, I'll go to the nearest hardware store and *I will buy some bricks and mortar!* Then, I will come right back and build you a nice fireplace, right in front of your bed! OK! And if I have one brick left over, do you know what you can do with it? I'll tell you what you can do with it!

At this point the entire audience is laughing. I explained that this is exactly what they would be doing if they were ever confronted with a similar situation. It's like I described earlier, with the toll booth incident. Your brain is no longer concentrating on negative thoughts. Your brain is somewhere else, laughing and thinking of something outrageous that you are currently doing. You have nipped a potentially negative and dangerous situation in the bud.

Even if your brain goes back to negative thoughts it won't be as overwhelming as it was before. Why? Because you've calmed down your nervous system to the point where you can take control. You are now in charge of your emotions.

In conclusion, I emphasized to the woman who asked the question that after she had calmed down she should approach the customer with whatever the scenario may be, i.e., *"I'm sorry. I don't know how this happened. I cannot find you a room with a fireplace this evening. But I notice that you are going to be here for three days. I'll tell you what I'll do. I'll give you the first night with our compliments, and tomorrow, at your convenience, someone will help you move your things to an upgraded suite with a fireplace, with no additional cost to you."*

I then addressed the entire group and stated that if the customer still isn't satisfied, at least you can say in all honesty that you tried everything in your power to help that customer. Whenever you deal with someone who is difficult, it's never a matter of who's right or who's wrong. It's about advantages and disadvantages. It's about happiness and inner peace opposed to anger and chaos. It's about coming from a state of love, not from a state of fear.

Most importantly, you do not sink to that person's level. Do not allow yourself to become victimized by someone else's attitude. Stop the snowball effect. Become energized and emotionally stable to deal with the next challenge, which will inevitably follow sooner or later. That's total power. That's total control. And all it takes is an imagination and the unleashing of your *humor being.*

105

Being victimized by someone else's bad attitude is an easy trap to fall into. Did you ever wake up in the morning in a really good mood? You don't know why but your feeling incredibly positive. Every aspect of your life seems wonderful. It's just a great day to be alive. Even your problems seem manageable and under control. Then somewhere along the course of your carefree day you are confronted by someone who has just stepped out from the deep, dark abyss of the *Negative Zone!* It can be your spouse, complaining about work or the children. Perhaps it's a friend telling you how his world is falling apart. Maybe it's your mother rambling on about her aches and pains or how she is never appreciated.

The point is, there were probably many times in your life when you allowed someone else's bad mood or negative attitude to ruin your day. And, you probably weren't even aware of what was happening. When you fall victim to these energy-suckers you are thereby granting them permission to regulate your happiness. You are also giving your personal power away. I find it absolutely amazing how someone's negative energy can affect almost everyone they come in contact with. I see it in airports, traffic jams, malls, supermarkets, and sporting events. I even witnessed someone's bad mood just about ruin an entire wedding reception.

We need to learn how to defend ourselves from the energy-suckers of the world. In situations like these, we need to call upon our *humor being* to the rescue.

106

A few years ago, I was speaking in the Midwest. I needed to stock up on some paper and other writing accessories, so I drove to a nearby K-Mart store. As I proceeded to purchase my goods, I noticed that there was only one register open, so I took my place at the end of a long line. While waiting, I heard the people in line mumbling something about the attitude of the young woman working the register. As I proceeded closer to the register, I understood what everyone was talking about. This woman did have a major attitude problem. But, what amazed me the most was how everyone else was making it their problem. The guy in back of me apparently found the need to add more fuel to the fire by venting loud enough for everyone to hear, "*Who does she think the is? I'm going to go over there and give her a piece of my mind!*" I'm thinking, "*Oh this is great. Somebody with no mind at all is going to give somebody else a piece of it.*" At that point, I noticed that everyone was feeding off of everyone else's negativity.

Now I guess my *humor being* was at an all time high that day. Because right in the middle of this negative frenzy, I took off my shoe, put it by my ear, and said (in a voice like Maxwell Smart from the old television series, "Get Smart") "*Hello Chief.* (Everyone in line just stared at me) *Yes, this is Max. Well, I'm at K-Mart and apparently the woman behind the register is a spy. How can I tell? She has a* **bug up her butt!**" There wasn't a person in that line who wasn't filled with tears of laughter. In fact, the guy behind me said, *"Hey, can I use your shoe? I have to call my wife!"*

What an amazing turn of events. One moment everyone was wallowing in negativity. The next moment they were all laughing. The woman behind the counter, she didn't get it at all. In fact, she was more upset then she was before. She looked at me and said, *"That is so stupid! A grown man talking to his shoe. There's no phone in there!"*

I learned a very important lesson that day. Some people take their jobs and their lives too seriously. They refuse to acknowledge that they have a sense of humor. State troopers refuse to acknowledge that they have a sense of humor. Below is a list of the top five things you should never say to a state trooper.

1. **State Trooper:** *Can I see your license and registration please?*
    Wrong Response: *Sure, you want to hold my beer?!*

2. **State Trooper:** *Didn't you see that stop sign?*
    Wrong Response: *Yeah, I saw it. I just didn't see you hiding behind it!*

3. **State Trooper:** *Are you drinking?*
    Wrong Response: *I don't know. Are you buying?*

4. **State Trooper:** *Well, it looks like I'm going to have to give you a ticket for speeding.*
    Wrong Response: *Well, could you make it quick? It's pretty apparent that I'm in a hurry.*

5. **State Trooper:** *How come you didn't stop when I was chasing you?*
    Wrong Response: *Well, a few years ago my wife ran away with a state trooper, and I thought you were trying to return her!*

FROM KLUTZ TO HERO

Awhile back I was at Hartsfield Atlanta Airport. I was patiently waiting to board a plane that was already forty-five minutes late. (Oh gee, what else is new?) An announcement was made informing us that the plane couldn't take off until the flight crew arrived. Now, I'm not an expert, but I thought that was a good reason not to take off.

After waiting another twenty minutes, the flight attendants and the co-pilot boarded the plane. But the captain was nowhere to be seen. I glanced over my shoulder and noticed that one gate away was our pilot. He was walking very fast and pulling along one of those typical pieces of luggage with the pull-up handle and wheels. Excusing himself as he turned into the gate area someone yelled out, *"Hey, Bill, you finally made it."*

As he turned to respond to the person who yelled at him, he walked into and knocked over a garbage can. You could see the humiliation on his face as he knelt down to pick up the scattered debris. Being the Good Samaritan that I am, I decided to give the poor guy a hand with his mess. He looked at me and said, *"I guess I didn't see it."*

109

I smiled, while to myself I thought, *"Oh my God. He's flying the plane!"*

He stood up, straightened out his uniform, thanked me and proceeded to board the plane. But, when he reached behind himself to grab the handle of his luggage, his arm hit a woman who was eating an ice cream cone. Notice I said was *eating* an ice cream cone. In a matter of seconds she was *wearing* it. At this point, dozens of people are staring at what seemed like a classic vaudeville act in the making. To tell you the truth I don't know who was getting most of the attention, the pilot, who was turning five shades of red and trying to apologize profusely, or the woman who was wiping ice cream from her face and dress, and trying desperately to control her temper.

After a few moments, which must have seemed like an eternity to him, the captain composed himself as best he could and proceeded toward the doorway to board the plane. Now, I don't know what compelled him, I guess he felt the need to look back to see if the woman was all right. This, of course was his last mistake, and perhaps biggest. As he turned, he walked into an airport cart. Somehow the cuff of his pants got stuck on the wheel.

I could only imagine the thoughts that were running through his head, as he stood there dumbfounded at this new predicament. I watched, as he shook his head in disbelief. He took a deep breath, yanked his cuff free, lost his balance, and fell onto the floor. At this point the entire gate area was watching him. There was a moment of awkward silence. You could have heard a pin drop. He waited a few seconds, picked himself up, and without missing a beat said, *"It's okay. I know what you're thinking. But I fly a lot safer than I walk!"*

That is emotional stability. With one humorous outburst this pilot relinquished all the negative thoughts that everyone had of him.

At one point everyone (including me) was looking at this guy as if he was a klutz. But by allowing his *humor being* to take over, he went from a klutz to a hero. I kid you not when I say hero. As soon as he spoke those words, *"I fly a lot safer than I walk,"* everyone immediately started to laugh and cheer. It was comic relief. People stood and applauded. Some whistled, patted him on the shoulders, and shook his hand. And he responded by taking, not one, but many bows.

Then the ticket agent got in on the fun. She opened up the door for him and escorted him down the gateway. The whole time he kept turning around to face the crowd, while tipping his hat and saying, *"Thank you! Thank you very much! You're beautiful! Thank you!"* For a minute I think he thought he was Elvis. This guy did everything but sign autographs.

When the plane took off he made an announcement. *"This is your captain. I just want to inform everyone that I'm sitting down and everything is okay. I'm not getting up for*

111

anything. I have to use the lavatory, but don't worry. I can wait until we land." I remember thinking that if there was ever an emergency on that plane he would be the person I would want in charge. How he dealt with the situation proved to me that he had emotional stability.

It's times like this when I am truly amazed at how powerful we can be when we allow our *humor beings* to take control. And that's exactly what it is, total control. I can't help but wonder what would have happened had he let that entire experience affect his emotional well being. I wonder if you, the reader know how blessed it truly is to have such control. Humor is a gift from God. Your *humor being* is God working through you to hold you up when you are about to fall.

High Points to Remember

ℝ If your day at work isn't going as planned or if the workload is becoming overload, stop and know you have a choice. Then, choose the way that will ground you to a foundation of emotional stability.

ℝ When you say that someone or some situation has caused you to become upset, you have given your personal power away. You are admitting that you are not in control of your life.

ℝ Anecdotal mimicry is a wonderful way to deal with overload and irate people. It will leave you feeling energized and emotionally stable. And all it takes is the unleashing of your *humor being*.

Chapter Eight
In the Spirit of Love

In such a short time our humor beings took us from a place of pain and uncertainty, to a place with inner peace and hope. Laughter made us realize that throughout our journeys there are no good-byes, only good memories.

One night I was on the phone talking to my friend Jeff. We were discussing the progress of my book. He suggested the book needed the story of a celebrity who had used their sense of humor as a tool to help them overcome a major challenge. I told him that was a good idea and tomorrow I would put an ad in the classifieds:

> Wanted! Famous person who overcame a major challenge or tragedy in their life by using sense of humor as tool to help them confront their fear.

When I hung up the phone, I thought about Jeff's sug-
gestion. He was right. Someone with a well-known name
would add an interesting twist to my book. I knew some
famous people, but none with the criteria I was looking
for. So I did what I usually do when I want something to
manifest into my life, I prayed and meditated. I asked God
that if this book needed the testimony of someone famous,
let our paths meet as soon as possible.

The next morning I was sitting in first class on a flight
to Nashville, Tennessee. An older gentleman approached
me and asked if I would mind switching seats so that he
and his wife could sit together. I obliged and moved up to
the first row aisle seat. Standing in the row adjacent to
mine was a very attractive woman wearing sunglasses.
She was talking to two distinguished-looking men who
(as I overheard from their conversation) were from MCA
Records. I didn't know exactly what they were talking
about, but it was obvious it was funny. The laughter was
non-stop. Laughter is contagious and I soon found myself
laughing, even though I didn't know what was being said.

We were ready for take-off and the woman with sunglasses sat down next to me. She put her boarding pass on
the armrest and I glanced at the name. As I had thought,
it was Naomi Judd. I smiled, shook my head and thought,
*"God, you never cease to amaze me. I know I wanted an
answer as soon as possible, but you really didn't have to work
that fast!"* I knew Naomi Judd had overcome a life-threatening illness, although I wasn't sure what it was.

I looked over and told her how much I enjoyed her work. I do. It wasn't a line. I may be from New York but I love country music! In fact, I write country music, but that's another story. She smiled and said, *"Thank you."* I introduced myself and it was the beginning of a wonderful conversation.

She told me that she spoke to groups throughout the country on health and spirituality. I said that I spoke to groups on how a sense of humor can change one's perspective of a fearful or a negative situation and give them the hope that is needed to perform miracles in their lives.

I knew that hit a sensitive spot, because she straightened up in her seat and said, *"What a wonderful subject."* The conversation continued, with both of us sharing stories and exchanging material from our speeches and seminars.

Eventually she told me about her life-threatening ordeal with contracting Hepatitis C. Apparently she was infected by pricking her finger with a needle years ago, when she was working as a nurse. She was diagnosed in 1990, but a liver biopsy showed that she had contracted the disease six years earlier. Doctors didn't give her very long to live.

I asked if humor helped her in any way to release the fear. She laughed, reached down and grabbed hold of a big leather bag, and pulled out a whoopee cushion and other humorous paraphernalia. *"Steve,"* she said, *"I'm*

*known as the Goofiest Woman In Country Music, and I'm
proud of it!"*

I was intrigued by the excitement that radiated from
her. At that moment I saw the child within the woman. I
remember thinking to myself, *"This is indeed an individual
who enjoys life to the fullest."*

Our conversation took on a more serious tone. She
stated that being sick was not her style. She hated being in
public in such a weak condition, so she instinctively relied
on her sense of humor. She felt the need to be around
people who could make her laugh. When she arrived at
the world-famous Mayo Clinic she was weak and scared.
They put her into a wheelchair and told her she was going
to the Admitting Office. Her reply was, *"You can take me
where you want, but I ain't admittin to nothin'!"*

There were times when Naomi felt that the life she
once loved so very much was dwindling away. But she
kept reaching for some kind of hope, an open window
with a light shining through. At one point, she met with a
new doctor for a second opinion. *"Your enzymes are higher
than ever,"* he said, with all the warmth of a glacier. *"The
active inflammation going on in your liver is destroying the
heptic cells. Now, these dead cells will turn into scar tissue
called cirrhosis. The damage is irreversible. Cirrhosis usually
turns into cancer, but before that, various parts of the liver
will begin shutting down. So it's hard to say which one will
actually be your demise."*

118

Her response was, *"How about them Dodgers?"* When the doctor said he needed to see her back in a week she said, *"Nope. You shoved me out of an airplane at 35,000 feet without giving me anything to break my fall. I'm going to find a doctor who will give me a parachute. It's called Hope."*

It was this type of attitude and quick wit that kept Naomi Judd from falling apart. It helped her control the fear that was trying to consume her. She told me that her sense of humor somehow always managed to re-connect her to her spiritual side. It was that connection that gave her hope to move forward in spite of fear. Hope was her constant companion. Humor was her shield. Together they helped her derail fear and to embrace the power of love.

Her innate ability to laugh in the face of fear is what aided in giving her the courage to carry on, even when the odds were against her. As she said to me so eloquently, *"I have a hitch in my giddy-up but I'm still a goin'."*

This is the attitude we all need to succeed and to enjoy ourselves on all levels of life. This, my friends, is the attitude humor can give us. It can give us the hope we need to turn a dismal situation around.

Let's face it, we will always have challenges. There will always be hard times and problems to solve. That's why we're here. If there is anything I've learned about our existence on this planet it is that everyone has his or her cross in life to bear. It's how we carry the cross that makes the difference and how we carry the cross is determined by the choices we make.

We must all get away from the preconceived idea that life is supposed to be easy. It's this belief that makes life frustrating and unfulfilling. In his book, *The Road Less Traveled*, Dr. Scott Peck writes, "Life is difficult."

When I read that I said, *"Duh! I know it's difficult. That's why I bought the book!"*

Dr. Peck also says that once we admit to ourselves that life is difficult, then our lives will become easier—because we won't have any preconceived ideas that we are lacking in any way.

I agree with Dr. Peck. Life is difficult. But I would like to add that sometimes we make our lives more difficult than they have to be. There are things that we can do to ourselves or for ourselves that can propel us into healthier states of mind, so we can deal with our difficulties more easily.

In her book, *Love Can Build A Bridge*, Naomi Judd says, *"Love is the greatest healing power all. There is nothing that comes close."* She also says, *"Hope is a gift we give to ourselves. It remains when all else is gone. It guides us beyond doubt and keeps us from sinking in our fears. It helps us picture the way we want things to be, so we can bring them about."*

I agree. *Love* is the greatest healing power of all. *Hope* is a gift we give to ourselves. It remains with us when all else is gone. Our *sense of humor* is also a gift. It, too, is filled with unlimited healing power. But as with love and hope, it is something we must choose to let into our lives. If we choose to view our problems, challenges and even our tragedies from a humorous perspective, we can prevent fear and negative emotions from controlling our destiny.

If hope was Naomi Judd's parachute, then humor was the force that helped her take that leap of faith; and love was the foundation she landed on. With these dynamics working within you, you can overcome insurmountable odds in your life. But, it's a matter of choice. It's always a matter of what you choose to believe.

So often we say we want to fulfill our dreams. We want success and happiness; yet we choose thoughts and behaviors and take actions that are counterproductive. They give us the complete opposite of what we want. I believe it is essential for us to understand that throughout our journey every thought we have, all of our beliefs and every action we take comes from two primary emotions: love or fear. They are pure energy of the soul and are at opposite ends from each other. All other emotions or ideas derive from these two. All decisions that are made come from the energy of love or fear, regardless if they are decisions about business, education, politics, domestic and foreign policy, religion, our social lives, or our relations with family, friends, coworkers, and strangers.

Fear and love cannot be experienced at the same time.

If fear, or negative emotions of any kind, consumes you, you have pushed love aside. If you are experiencing love and inner peace, you have cast out fear as a result of the choices you have made. If you are aware of this you can then make a conscious effort to make your choices from a state of love.

When I say love, I'm talking about your lifeline, your connection to your higher self. I'm talking about the power that ignites creativity—the energy that is a part of you, that makes you feel moments of perfection and total bliss. I'm talking about the unconditional force that connects you and enables you to communicate with God.

In other words, when you are connected to love, your life works. When you are not connected to love, your life doesn't work. When you are connected to love, you simply feel good about yourself inside, in spite of what happens on the outside. You are able to deal with challenges and make decisions. It means waking up with energy and enthusiasm and going to sleep with peace of mind. It means feeling positive about you, regardless of any mistakes or failures. It means feeling confident and complete when things aren't going right. It means having respect, compassion, and forgiveness for yourself and for others.

Being connected to love can put you in what author Mihaly Csikszentmihalyi calls *flow*. When you are in a state of *flow*, you are relishing the moment, free from worry or any outside force, because you are centered on love. From the energy of love comes faith, hope, inner peace, joy, bliss, compassion and happiness. They are all components that make up the spirit of love. Without these wonderful and miraculous qualities our lives would be in complete shambles.

Making choices from a state of love brings in the support of the universe. You release an energy that will knock down the walls of fear and negativity. When you choose from a state of love you rise up to any challenge. Even the impossible takes on a magical, healing quality. Trying to acquire more love shouldn't be your goal; because you were born with this power. No one has more than anyone else. Your goal should be to keep fear and all negative emotions from separating you from your connection to love. When you unleash your *humor being*, you will set forth an energy that radiates hope, which can deliver you from your fears and connect you to the power of love. Only when you are connected to love can you believe that somehow, someway, some good will come out of even the most tragic situation.

Viktor Frankl reflects on the true power of the spirit of love when he describes the experiences that he had in Auschwitz. In the midst of pain, hunger, torture, disease and utter desolation, it was the image of his wife's face in the sky and the conversations he had with her image that gave him the willpower to survive.

Dr. Frankl says that love is the ultimate and highest goal to which man can aspire. In the middle of utter desolation he clung to the image of his wife. He didn't know if she was alive or not. He only knew one thing, which he learned so well, "Love goes very far beyond the physical person of the beloved. It finds its deepest meaning in the spiritual being, the inner self." Whether or not his wife was actually present, whether or not she was still alive, somehow ceased to be important.

> I did not know whether my wife was alive, and I had no means of finding that out; but at that moment it ceased to matter. There was no need for me to know, nothing could touch the strength of my love, my thoughts and the image of my beloved. Had I known that my wife was dead, I think that I would still have given myself undisturbed by that knowledge, to the contemplation of her image, and that my mental conversation with her would have been just as vivid and just as satisfying. *'Set me like a seal upon thy heart, love is as strong as death.'*

These words unequivocally show the true power of the *spirit of love*. You can feel it long after the person is gone. I would like to share with you a particular experience I had when humor rekindled the same spirit of love that Viktor Frankl is talking about.

❧ In the Spirit of Love ❧

A Smile From Within

Years ago I attended the wake and funeral services of a friend who was killed in a car crash. He was in his early thirties and was loved by everyone who had the pleasure of knowing him. I had been to many wakes and funeral services throughout the course of my life. The causes of death ranged from drug or alcohol abuse, accident, suicide, sickness, violence and old age. There was something special, however, about this particular situation. An awareness came over me that caused me to view the losses in my life from a different perspective.

When the funeral services were over a group of us met at a relative's house. As you would expect, people were still wiping tears and consoling one another. Some shook their heads in disgust at the unfair twist that life had bestowed upon them. Others questioned God for taking the life of someone who had so much more to give.

Across the room I overheard parts of a story being told about my friend. I noticed that a few people were laughing. Then someone else joined in on the conversation, and more people started to laugh. Before long everyone in this room was laughing, reminiscing, and telling stories about my friend. Then, in the midst of all the laughter, I had a strange uplifting feeling come over me. I realized I was no longer grieving over my friend. In fact, at that moment, I felt as if a part of him was still with me—and always would be. The only way I can describe this feeling is that it was like a *smile from within*. It was a feeling of total peace and acceptance.

Before I go any further with this story, I want to discuss the importance of crying and mourning over our losses. Crying and mourning are good. They, too, are gifts from God. They are natural releases which our bodies need in order for us to heal emotionally, mentally, physically and spiritually.

Sometimes, however, we grieve and mourn too much. By doing this we tend to concentrate on our losses. This can lead to unhealthy feelings of helplessness, despair and a sense of feeling victimized or cheated. These feelings keep the spirit of love and its healing power from entering. If we don't allow love to enter, we leave ourselves wide open for fear to take control, leaving us in states of anger, guilt, blame and resentment.

I found that grieving and crying reinforced the fact that my friend was gone and had died a horrible senseless death. But when stories were being told about him and everyone was laughing, it somehow lifted us up and delivered us from our pain. It made us feel close to him, like a part of him was still with us. In fact, his wife said, *"You know, it's funny. I miss him and always will. But right now I feel like a part of him is with me, and always will be."* Then she paused and said, *"It's as if he's saying to us right now, to all of us, that 'It's OK. I'm OK. Everything is as it should be. I will always be with you.'"* Of course when she said that we all started crying again. But this time they were tears of joy and hope.

You see, Viktor Frankl is right. Love goes far beyond the physical person of the beloved. It finds its deepest meaning in the spiritual being, the inner self. Whether or not my friend was alive didn't seem to matter at the moment. The only thing that mattered was the powerful feeling we were all experiencing. We were celebrating and embracing the spirit of our love for him and the spirit of his love for us. It was our ability to laugh and reminisce about the good times that ignited the spirit. In such a short time our *humor beings* took us from a place of pain and uncertainty to a place of inner peace and hope. Laughter made us realize that throughout our journeys there are no good-byes, only good memories. The spirit lives on.

All of us felt that smile from within that day. It's a smile of the spirit that derives from the profound love that Viktor Frankl explains so eloquently. This smile is truly a feeling of hope that transcends time. I believe it's God's way of saying that some of us are going to get hit hard throughout our journey. It may be the parting or death of a loved one. You may become physically or mentally handicapped as a result of an accident or illness. You may lose your job, or your house, or you may come across financial disaster.

Whatever the loss, there is always hope. For that loss is only on the physical realm. The spirit of the deceased will never die! The spirit that directed you to acquire that job will never die! The spirit that drove you to purchase or to build your house will never die! And the spirit that guided you to financial success and to live your dream will never die! The spirit that constitutes who you really are never dies! It will always be with you. You were born with it. Its energy will continue to radiate long after you're gone.

It is a truly wise person who knows that he or she has a choice on how to deal with life's challenges. It is an even wiser person who chooses to use the tools that can help ease their pain and guide them to a healthier, more productive outcome. Your smile from within is of the spirit of love. It can't be taken away. You can't give it away. You need only be aware of its presence and choose to embrace its magical healing qualities. When you do, miracles will blossom within you and around you.

HIGH POINTS TO REMEMBER

৯ From the energy of love comes faith, hope, inner peace, joy, bliss, compassion and happiness. Without these wonderful and miraculous qualities your life would be in a shambles.

৯ Making choices from a state of love brings in the support of the universe. You release an energy that will knock down the walls of negativity.

৯ When you unleash your *humor being* you set forth an energy that radiates hope, which will deliver you from your fears and connect you to the power of love. Only when you are connected to love can you believe that somehow, some way, some good will come out of even the most tragic situation.

Chapter Nine

Fear and the Destroyers of the Spirit

*When you choose to view your experiences
from the perception of lessons to be learned, it
not only gives your life meaning, but you
will find that every experience was necessary
for you to grow and move on—even if it was
painful at the time.*

I was sitting backstage at the Sands Hotel. Woody Harrelson of *Cheers* was hosting the show. He approached me and asked how I wanted to be introduced. I thought for a moment and then said, *"Tell them that you're going to bring up a guy who was voted 'Least Likely to Succeed' in his senior class in high school. Now he's here in Atlantic City at the Sands Hotel filming a ShowTime special!"*

As Woody walked away I wondered why I told him to

say that. Then it hit me. It was the first time in my life I believed dreams could come true.

When I was voted "Least Likely to Succeed" in high school I thought it was a big joke. Now I realize it was that type of negative labeling that molded the direction for most of my life. It instilled so much fear in me that I was afraid to try. My philosophy was *"If you don't try, you can't fail."* This was the only way I knew how to avoid the pain of rejection and failure. I ignored or ran away from many opportunities. Even when I tried to succeed at something, all I needed was to make just one mistake or to receive a bit of criticism from someone to reinforce the belief that I was not good enough.

I remember the empty feeling I had in high school as I sat as a spectator, watching my friends play football and perform in the school play. I knew I had the talent to participate, but the words that had become so familiar kept echoing in my head, *"If you don't try, you can't fail."* My fears began to snowball and I took them into my adult life. As a result, I felt victimized and cheated. My anger grew and I started blaming others for my plight. Why was everyone getting what I wanted? Why were my peers climbing up the ladder of success? Why wasn't opportunity knocking at my door? I never realized it was knocking and that I was just too afraid to open it.

The only release I had was when I was onstage, with a microphone in my hand, making people laugh. As I look back, I can see that I was lost, confused, and just waiting for someone or something to show me the way. For years I repressed my feelings with alcohol and drugs. I was playing the part of the funnyman who didn't seem to have a care in the world. As I said earlier, I used my sense of humor as a blanket to pull over my head, like a child does when he's in bed alone in the dark, so the monsters won't get him. My monsters came to me in many disguises, but they all derived from the same source of energy—FEAR.

The opposite of love is fear. Fear is where the ego originates. It's the manifestation of negative thinking by choice. The ego is constantly reminding you that you are not good enough and that you are lacking in some way and need more. It keeps you in a constant state of turmoil, competition, and chaos.

Anger, hatred, guilt, blame, jealousy, envy, doubt, resentment, depression, worry, despair, and all other negative emotions are derived from fear. I call all of these negative emotions the Destroyers Of The Spirit because that's what they do. They knock the love right out of you. If your life isn't working right now on any level, personally or professionally, it's because of one or more of these Destroyers Of The Spirit. They are responsible for keeping you from your dreams and true potential.

I don't care who you are or how much money you make, you cannot be truly successful unless you know that you have the power to control your fears and the

Destroyers Of The Spirit from robbing you from the quality of peace and happiness you desire. Knowing you have the power is not enough. You must also know that you have a choice, and then choose to utilize that power in a way so that it represents your higher self, despite the fear and its limiting beliefs.

Later on in this chapter I will show you how your *humor being* can help you to unleash this power and confront your fears; but for now, let's just be concerned with where our fears come from.

One of the devastating consequences of the Destroyers Of The Spirit is that they eat at the core of your intuitive self. When you were a child your intuitive self was at its peak. That's when you were most carefree and went with the flow. As children our imaginations are very sharp and we are in our most natural state, free from fear of failure, rejection, and making mistakes.

Unfortunately, our childhood is when we are the most sensitive and crave acceptance and approval. As children our natural talents and abilities should be nurtured and cared for, so that we can show our true magnificence. Too often our talent, along with our imagination and our intuitive self, are smothered by the wrath of fear and the Destroyers Of The Spirit and the limiting beliefs that they harbor, causing us to stifle our true self and to seek approval from others. The real danger sets in when we leave home and try to make it on our own. Unaware, we carry with us many of our unresolved negative labels and limiting beliefs. If these issues aren't dealt with, they will manifest as a series of problems on all levels of our life.

Time Travel

In order for us to stop fear and the Destroyers Of The Spirit from controlling our lives, I believe that it is a good idea to first find out where they came from. We must be able to step back into our past and take a good look at what happened to us when we lived at home, where we fit in at school, and how we interacted with adults and peers. Then we must weed out what was stopping us from growing, replant ourselves, and nurture our soul so we can grow to our full potential.

Traveling into the past is a wonderful way to discover where your fears and limiting beliefs came from. All you need to do is to sit in a quiet place or go for a walk and let your mind travel through your past. When I time travel I try to go back as far as I can. Usually things start coming into focus around my early years of grade school.

I find it beneficial to have some kind of sequential order when I time travel. For example, I allow myself to travel through the events of first grade to second grade, then second grade to third and so on. I actually witness how I interacted with my peers, teachers, parents, and other authority figures. This not only enables me to understand why or where my negative patterns and fears evolved, but it also shows me how they eventually created my reality.

As you journey into your past you will be confronted by your fears. You will hear what was said to you. You will see what was done to you. And you will experience how you were treated by and how you responded to authority figures. There will be times when you will relive some very powerful experiences. Some will hit you like a tidal wave of emotions.

You might hear a teacher tell you that you'll never amount to anything. You might witness how your artistic ability was stifled because a parent or other authority figure was constantly telling you how to be practical. *"Get your head out of the clouds and stop being a foolish day-dreamer." "Let me tell you what you need."*

Some of you may relive many painful experiences of never fitting in with your peers, or remember how you had to conceal your true feelings so you would be accepted. A part of you may want to react with anger, revenge, blame, or guilt. This is the ego telling you to respond with the only way it knows how—from fear. Resist the urge to pass judgment and embrace your emotions, no matter how painful they are.

When I was growing up I had a lot of athletic ability, but I was afraid to compete because I thought I would fail. I cared too much about what others thought. In eighth grade I had the courage to try out for the football team. I knew I had what it took to make the team, but my fears got the best of me. During practice I kept falling down and dropping passes. I can't tell you how many times the ball bounced off my head. I was so concerned about what the coaches and other players where thinking I couldn't concentrate on what needed to be done.

One night during supper my dad asked me how practice had gone. I said it went okay and tried to avoid the subject. I knew I was nervous, because I asked my mom to pass the spinach, and I hate spinach.

Then my brother Rocky said, *"Hey Dad, what does it mean when the coach says that a member of the team is a fish?"*

My father laughed and said, *"It means that you're clumsy and fall down a lot."*

My brother said, *"Oh, because that's what the coach said Steven is."*

Both my father and brother thought it was real funny and had a good laugh. Oh I laughed too, but inside I was humiliated and embarrassed. I pretended it didn't bother me and spent the rest of the evening in my room.

Now I could have gone to practice the next day and showed the coach and everyone else that I wasn't a fish. I could have showed them how talented I was, but I didn't. My fear got the best of me. The next morning I arrived at school earlier than usual and I left my equipment in front of the coach's office. That was the last time I ever tried out for a sport or any other event during my high school years. Time travel has allowed me to see similar patterns and various reasons as to why I have limiting beliefs, where they came from and how they may be affecting my choices in the present.

It is important to remind yourself that your goal and only purpose for time travel is to understand where your fears and limiting beliefs came from. You might remember that someone did something that made you feel uncomfortable or caused you to feel grief or pain; but then you must let it go. Once you come to the realization that you are responsible for everything that happens to you, then you are on your way to free yourself from your past.

Know that you have the power of choice. The past and anyone in it cannot hurt you, unless you choose to let them. When you choose to view all of your experiences from the perception of lessons to be learned, it not only gives your life meaning but you will find that every experience was necessary for you to grow and move on—even if it was painful at the time.

Often when a traumatic event happens we find it difficult to understand the significance. We want to lash out and accuse. But if we search and try to understand, we can see how that event caused our soul to grow. It is the embracing of our joys and happiness, as well as our pain and heartache, that enables soul-growth.

LETTING GO OF PAST LIMITATIONS

The way to embrace your past experiences without judgment or regret is to allow your *humor being* to play the role of an observer. Remember, your *humor being* is of your higher self. It has many healing qualities, all of which are centered on helping you soothe your very being. As an observer your *humor being's* function is to stand outside of a particular experience and simply examine it, without distinguishing good from bad or right from wrong. It just observes, as only your higher self can, in a peaceful, non-judgmental, and compassionate way.

Often when you time travel your inner dialogue may challenge the two parts of you that are in conflict with each other. For example, when I time travel I sometimes notice that one side of me is angry or upset and wants to lash out and pass judgment for some pain that was bestowed upon me, yet the other side of me wants to forgive the person that caused the pain. Then the other side says, *"Why should I forgive after what was done to me?"* And so on. This inner dialogue can be exhausting, to say the least.

Here's where your *humor being* can be very effective. First, as an observer, it becomes a mediator between your inner dialogue. It reminds you that your only purpose for time travel is to view your past experiences as they truly are—lessons to be learned. If you use your imagination and allow your *humor being* free reign you can relive the entire experience from a humorous perspective.

In other words, you have the power to rewrite your tragedy into a comedy. You are the writer, director and editor. That means you can rewrite, redirect, and edit any part of your past. This is a tremendous opportunity to keep fear and anger from controlling your life.

For example, when I reviewed my eighth-grade football experience, initially I allowed my *humor being* to stand back and observe the entire experience. This decision to view the incident from a distance put me in control, because I allowed my higher self to stand apart from my ego and the pain associated with the entire experience.

When you observe, you acquire understanding and compassion as to how and why the situation happened the way it did.

Then I decided to have some fun. I allowed my *humor being* to rewrite my entire eighth-grade football experience. First I re-directed my practice and made myself the star in an old-fashioned football film. The entire event happened in fast motion. I even added some honky-tonk piano music in the background. (Hey, this is my movie; I'll do what I want!) I saw myself falling down and dropping passes, balls bouncing off my head and guys three times my size chasing me around the field. It looked like I was directing and starring in a Charlie Chaplin movie.

Viewing the experience this way was very reassuring. In fact, it was a relief to know I could laugh at a part of myself and my past that had caused me so much pain. I even directed myself to walk up to the coach and say, *"The joke is on you pal, because you will never know how good I really am!"*

I found this way of viewing this experience so empowering that I decided to let my *humor being* go a step further. I cut to the scene where my brother told my father that the coach said I was a fish. Only this time I was a fish. I mean my body was mine, but my head was that of a fish. There I was, sitting at the dinner table saying, *"Excuse me. Can you please pass the worms? And by the way, what's wrong with being a fish? I resent that!"*

This is one of the many ways your *humor being* can perform miracles. In your mind's eye you are now viewing a painful experience as non-threatening. You are laughing off the fear and anger that has been controlling your life. This helps you to back away from the pain. And don't be surprised if you hear yourself say, *"This is wonderful! This is great! I can deal with this! Now, let me see what seed of good I can find in this adversity from my past. How has or how can this experience help me grow?"*

Your *humor being* helps you understand that all of the terrible things that happen to you are really seeds for all of the great things that eventually blossom. That's why it is important to bless and not curse your past experiences, for they are lessons that determine who you really are. All of your past, present, and future challenges are lessons. You need them in order to graduate and move on to the next step on your journey in the school of life. Each circumstance is a gift and each experience is a hidden treasure. Even a tragedy is an opportunity to grow. Your *humor being* simply helps you make decisions so you can move to the next level—without your past limitations.

We must all realize that negative labels are not who we are. They are just the opinions and verbal garbage of others. Don't let your past experiences dictate what you can or can't become. Make a stand and laugh out loud in the face of fear. Reclaim your power and make a conscious effort to move forward and dare to be who you really are.

Sometimes it's wise to just stop the world and get off. Take time out to rekindle your intuitive powers. Go inside for the answers. Ask yourself, *"What's important for me in my life? What will it take to make me happy? What do I need? What do I want to happen?"* I place the emphasis on *I* and *me* because the most important gift you could ever give yourself is to be who you are—not who others think you are—not what others think you should be. I'm not saying that you shouldn't listen to the opinions of others. I'm not saying that you shouldn't take advice. All I'm saying is to be aware. Know that it is your life. You owe it to yourself to weigh out the opinions of others.

More often than not it is during the sensitive and most

vulnerable period of our childhood that our maps are charted for our life's journey. Sometimes all it takes is just one negative remark, especially from someone with authority, to start a young life on a course filled with fear, doubt, and hopelessness. That's why I stress to parents and teachers to be careful what they say to children and adolescents. The wrong choice of words can lead to character assassination.

I'm reminded of the saying, *"Sticks and stones will break my bones but words will never hurt me."* This may be true if you are a mature adult, when you can rationally say these words are just the thoughts or opinions of someone else, and let them go. But one of the disadvantages of being a child is that your choices are very limited. The younger we are, the more limiting are the choices. For the most part children are at the mercy of the thoughts and opinions of their elders. In this respect, words can slowly destroy a child. If you get hit with a stick or a stone, eventually the pain subsides and the wounds heal. The wounds and scars caused by negative words that are bestowed upon children may never heal, and the fear, pain and limiting beliefs that are associated with the words can last a lifetime.

I THINK IT'S ABOUT FORGIVENESS

I remember another incident in eighth grade, when I was sitting with my parents in a guidance counselor's office.

We were there to review my curriculum for my remaining high school years and to prepare me for college. I was nervous, but very excited about fulfilling my dream of becoming a teacher. It was then that this guidance counselor told me that I didn't have what it took to go to college. He didn't even know my name or what I was all about. He never asked me about my dreams or aspirations. He just looked at a folder filled with papers and made his decision.

Now I know I wasn't the smartest kid in school. In fact, I really didn't try at all. But he never gave me a chance to speak. He never asked for my opinion. He just glanced over the papers in the file, looked at his watch and told me I wasn't smart enough to fulfill my dream. Perhaps he could have said something encouraging like, *"If you really want to go to college you're going to have to buckle down and study very hard."* He could have suggested special tutoring to help me through, but he didn't.

The real tragedy was that I believed him, and so did my mom and dad. They were from the old school of thought. They didn't know any better. We believed this man knew what he was talking about. I mean, he's an expert in his field. Look at his title—"Guidance Counselor." He must know what he's talking about. If he doesn't know, who does? It's what he gets paid for.

Not only did I allow this man to keep me from my dream of becoming a teacher, but to make a bad situation worse, I let him tell me what I was going to do with my life. He set up a curriculum for me in the business world. Oh how exciting! I had absolutely no idea what he was talking about as he rambled on about accounting and marketing. I thought marketing meant I was going to go food shopping. I'll never forget how I felt as I sat in this man's office, listening to him tell me I didn't have what it took to go to college. I was devastated, ashamed, and embarrassed. It was difficult for me to look at my parents. I felt like I let them down. At the age of 14 I was faced, again, with the harsh reality that dreams are for more fortunate people, and I definitely wasn't one of them.

Fortunately, this story has a happy ending. I did eventually go to college. And I graduated with honors. I also went on to teach and counseled high school students with behavioral problems. By the way, I was then teaching at the same school that I graduated from. Yes, that's right. The same district where the guidance counselor told me I didn't have what it took.

Believe me when I say this, college wasn't easy for me. As I look back, I find it absolutely astonishing how my negative labels were constantly coming out to haunt me. With every semester that passed and every course I took, my past experiences followed me like shadows.

Just recently, I decided to go time traveling once again and reviewed the whole guidance counselor scenario from a healthier perspective. I allowed my *humor being* to come to the rescue. I had a great deal of fun rewriting and redirecting this particular scene from my life!

First, I created two versions of me. So that you can have a better understanding we will call them the *8th Grade Me* and the *Now Me*. Only the *8th Grade Me* can see and hear the *now me*.

The scene begins with both sitting in the guidance counselor's office. The *Now Me* is informing the *8th Grade Me* about everything the counselor is going to say. But he urged me not to worry because I was going to live a wonderful life. He then went on to tell me all of my achievements up until the present moment.

We both just sat there with big grins on our faces. When the counselor was finally through mapping out my life he looked at me and said, *"What in the world have you been smiling at this entire time? This is serious stuff here. We're talking about your future."*

I jumped up and looked at my mom and dad. And then, I looked right at the counselor. Just as I was about to open my mouth, I heard the *Now Me* singing "My Way." Then my smile turned into a burst of laughter. I glanced at the *Now Me* and we both lost total control. The whole time the *Now Me* was saying, *"Go ahead. Tell him. Now's your chance!"*

The laughter subsided. I took a deep breath and looked right in the counselor's eyes and said, *"You've just spent the past half-hour telling me what I can and can't do with my life. You told me that I didn't have what it takes to go to college. You never asked me about my dreams. You didn't give me any hope at all. You never once thought about asking me for my opinion! But I'm going to give it to you anyway. Now I'm going to tell you what I'm going to do with my life."*

He looked as if he was about say something but I never gave him the chance. *"First of all,"* I said, *"I will go to college and I will graduate with honors. I will then go on to teach and counsel high school students. I will then leave the school system and go on to do something that many people say is one of the most difficult things to do, stand-up comedy. For 18 years, I will headline comedy clubs all over the country and other parts of the world. This will eventually lead me to star in many cable and network television shows.*

"The experiences I will have on the road will be more than I ever dreamed of. The people I will meet will fill my heart with love and compassion. The lessons I will learn will be my reward for not listening to people like you."

He then jumped up from his seat and tried to say something and I said, *"Shut up and sit down. I'm not finished yet, bub!* (Remember, this is my script. I can rewrite and redirect it any way I want!) *After 18 years as a successful comedian I will then make another major change. I will again follow my heart and enter the speaking forum. A vocation, mind you, that is considered the No. 1 fear by most people. It is at that point in my life; where I will create my own company called Laugh It Off Productions. I will have offices in Chicago and*

New York. As a speaker, all of my life lessons will be used to help others lead healthy and happy lives."

"Don't forget the book!" the *Now Me* yelled out.

"Oh", I said, *"I almost forgot. I will write a book that will get rave reviews. It will be called,* Becoming A Humor Being.*"*

I looked over at the *Now Me* who was smiling with admiration. My mom and dad were looking at me as if I were possessed. Then I turned to the counselor once more and said, *"Well, that's about all of the information I have about my life at this point in time. But you have to admit, Sparky, that ain't bad for a guy who doesn't seem to have what it takes!"*

I'm not sharing this story to put blame on the guidance counselor. In fact, I now view the entire experience as a lesson learned. My *humor being* helped me to realize that this person was probably doing his job the best or only way he knew how. I tell this story so that you can see once again how time travel works and how someone—especially someone with authority—can plant the seeds of negative labeling.

It is important you understand that no matter what has been said or done to you in your past, whether it was done intentionally or unintentionally, you have a choice on how to deal with it. You can both learn from and bless your past experiences and move on or you can curse your past and become a victim.

Remember the victim comes from fear. The victim is

the one who doesn't take responsibility and blames outside circumstances for his or her plight. Victims always
come up with a million excuses as to why their lives aren't
working. Victims never learn the lessons that the school of
life is trying to teach them. They keep reliving the same
experiences of unlearned lessons over and over again.
This, my friends, is a part of what hell is all about.

Putting the blame on others for your shortcomings
and heartache only delays the healing process. It keeps
you from moving on and graduating to the next step. You
must forgive others and yourself for all of the things that
were done to you or done by you. Think about this. It
doesn't make sense for you to deplete your valuable
energy and waste your time carrying heavy baggage filled
with unhealthy memories.

When you forgive someone you're not necessarily
doing it for the other person's sake. You're doing it for
your sake. You forgive so you can wake up every morning
and go to sleep every night without that knot in your
stomach. When you forgive you're not righting a wrong
or excusing what was done to you. Rather you are freeing
yourself from the pain, anger, and guilt that has been controlling your life and robbing you of the happiness you
desire.

You may say you have a right to be angry towards
someone who has done you harm, but you also have a
right to the ulcers, high blood pressure, headaches,

upset stomachs, and miserable existence that inevitably follow.

Singer-songwriter Don Henley says, *"Forgiveness is the heart of the matter."* These words hit the nail on the head. If we don't allow ourselves the luxury of forgiveness we thereby deny our connection to love.

Believe me when I say it took me most of my life to figure out I was and always will be responsible for my life. It doesn't matter now who said or did what to me. And it doesn't matter what I did or said to someone else. The only thing that is important is how I feel about it now.

As soon as I realized I was responsible for my success and happiness, and that I had a choice on how to deal with what happens to me, including my past, my entire attitude about my existence shifted. With this new sense of responsibility came the realization that my sense of humor can have a profound impact on my life.

I have found that humor and its by-product, laughter, are parts of us that come from pain. Someone said that if we could take a pill to release all of our negative thoughts and open us to the universe and its infinite supply of energy, we would express ourselves with total magnificence. Well, we may not have a pill to release our negative thoughts, but we do have tools that can help us. One of these tools is our sense of humor.

If fear, anger, guilt, blame, hatred, jealousy, envy, self-doubt, resentment, worry and despair are the Destroyers Of The Spirit, then your *humor being* is the Defender Of The Spirit, because it helps bring love, hope, inner peace, bliss, happiness, joy and compassion back into your life. Once you understand the nature behind this Defender Of The Spirit, then you can utilize its healing powers to free you from your fears and limiting beliefs—thereby untying your wings and enabling you to fly higher than you ever imagined.

HIGH POINTS TO REMEMBER

☙ The way to embrace your past experiences without judgment or regret is to allow your *humor being* to take on the role of an observer. The observer helps you view your past as lessons to be learned in the school of life.

☙ Use your imagination and allow your *humor being* free reign to relive the entire past experience from a humorous perspective. You have the power to rewrite, redirect, and edit your tragedy into a comedy.

☙ It is important to bless and not curse your past. Each experience is a hidden treasure. Even a tragedy is an experience to grow from. Your *humor being* simply helps you make decisions so you can move on to the next level, without your past limitations.

Chapter Ten
Embrace Change

*I believe that whenever a door is slammed
shut there is an open window with a light
shining through. That light is a ray of hope. I
call it "Saving Grace."*

One of our greatest challenges is to deal with the changes that occur in our lives. When I speak to a group, I inform them that one of their most powerful allies in embracing change is their *humor being*.

First, let's discuss why change is so difficult to accept and why we need to embrace change in order to live happy and successful lives.

Sometimes change comes by way of choice. Sometimes it is forced upon us by circumstances beyond our control. Either way, change is a part of life. It is necessary in order for us to grow to our full potential. Life is about experiencing, learning, growing, and becoming.

You cannot truly experience, you cannot learn, and you will not grow or become unless you allow yourself to embrace the changes throughout your journey. You cannot ignore change. You cannot fight it or make believe it's not taking place. And, you have to do more than just accept it.

When you allow yourself to embrace the changes in your life, you are thereby surrendering to a certain trust, an unshakable faith, that somehow, someway, some good will result from even the most tragic situation. As I look back at my life, I can see that every circumstance, especially the ones when I hit rock bottom, were nourishing to my soul.

When confronted with a challenge or facing a tragic situation, we stand alone at a fork in the road. We can choose to take the way most commonly traveled and complain, seek pity and rationalize our negative feelings. Those who choose this road set themselves up for failure and unhappiness, and will never reap the benefits that are hidden within each challenge. There are those, however, who choose to take the road that is seldom explored, and view each challenge as an opportunity in disguise. They embrace the changes in their lives by deciding to see the possibilities instead of concentrating on the loss and heartache.

Fear prohibits people from embracing change. Many people fear the unknown and will come up with all kinds of excuses in order to stay in their comfort zone. They panic at the thought of leaving the life they are used to, even if their present way of living is causing them pain and misery. There are those who stay in abusive relationships because the pain of leaving and starting a new life is more powerful than staying and taking the abuse.

Many people despise their jobs and complain every day. Yet as soon as they get fired or laid off, the first thing they say is, *"Oh my God! Why did this happen to me?"* Well, maybe it's the universe's way of saying *"Hello! This is your wake-up call! I knew you didn't like your job. I also knew you were stuck in your comfort zone and would never muster up enough courage to quit. Well, guess what? I just did you a favor. Now is your chance to do what you always wanted to do! Now you can embrace this change and go with the flow! Now you are open to a whole new world of possibilities! Now you can fulfill your dreams and start your own business, or go back to school and get that degree. Maybe now you can pursue something that will allow you to spend more time with your family or to enhance your artistic ability."*

My Heart's Desire

In the early 1990s, the once very lucrative comedy business was on a major decline. Clubs closed down throughout the country. Ironically, at this time, more comedians entered the already over-saturated market. Before, I had the luxury of choosing any club I wanted—at top pay.

155

Now, I was faced with the harsh reality of working any club that was open, with a substantial cut in pay. Work was hard to come by and the bills were getting tougher to pay.

It was very clear that the way of life I had come to know and love, the world that was so much a part of who I was, had changed drastically. Old fears I thought I had under control came back to haunt me. It took every ounce of energy for me to fight off the wrath of negative thinking.

None of these changes, however, compared with the changes that were taking place inside of me. I began to acquire a different set of values and beliefs. Many of the things I thought were important now seemed trivial. My desire, especially the need for fame and fortune, did not seem appealing or fulfilling anymore. I found that I was losing enthusiasm to have my own sitcom. Auditions were becoming a burden instead of something to look forward to.

Yes, I loved making people laugh, but it wasn't enough. Something inside was telling me I should be helping people in a more profound way.

I tried for the longest time to hide these changes. The more I suppressed these feelings, the more chaotic and frustrating my life became. My anger grew and I had very little patience with myself. For a time my life was just a series of going through the motions. No matter what I did or how hard I tried, my heart was not into it.

One thing was certain, I wasn't happy. In fact, I was the complete opposite. I was lost and depressed, and it didn't seem to be getting any better. The only thing that kept me above water was my wife's compassion, sense of humor, and her ability to put things into perspective.

All I knew was that I had dedicated a great part of my life to the world of stand-up comedy. I had made major sacrifices, and to admit to myself that I did not want it anymore was too much for me to deal with. My house was on Long Island, but my work demanded that I live in Los Angeles, where I rented an apartment with a friend. When I was not on the road working to pay bills, I was in Los Angeles, auditioning for television and radio commercials, sitcoms, and movies. In between, I would fly home and try to spend quality time with my family.

When I look back, I see that it was not so much that I was losing my passion for stand-up comedy and show business; it was more that I was being called to do something else. Occasionally, I would get these intuitive feelings. I call them silent voices of the soul. *"This is not what you want,"* or *"This is not what you are supposed to be doing with your life."*

In time, these feelings became stronger. But the stronger they became, the harder I tried to suppress them. I could not admit to myself that I had another calling. Not now, after so many years of dedication and hard work. The constant denial of my true feelings eventually turned my world into complete havoc, which is what happens when you consistently deny the calling of your soul. Unfortunately, it is something that is very easy to do.

The silent voice of your soul is your intuition, your higher self. It knows what you need to be happy. It shows you the way or your heart's desire. Your heart's desire is the urging of your soul that seeks self-recognition and expression. It does not speak to you in words, but in feelings. Although your intuition is very powerful, most of the time it speaks softly, between your thoughts. This is why meditation and quiet time alone are so important. They give you the opportunity to hear the silent voice of your soul and the message it brings.

When I tuned out the voice of my soul, I smothered my heart's desire. I left myself wide open for the loud, voice of the ego. *"There you go again. What is wrong with you? Most people know what they want at your age. Most people have direction and have established themselves. But no! Not you! Fifteen years in this business, and now you want to do something else. You did the same thing once before, remember? All those years of college, you taught and counseled kids, then quit and decided to go into show business. Let's not even talk about your personal relationships. Make up your mind! There are people depending on you!"*

The First Step

One day, after an audition, I returned to my apartment in Los Angeles. I was in a daze and I remember looking around and saying to myself that I did not belong there. Just then, my roommate said, *"Where do you want to go for dinner?"*

I said, *"Go where you want. I'm going back home to New York."*

"Why?" he said. *"They have great restaurants here!"*

I told him I was going home for good and that I would pay him for the rent until he found another roommate. He told me that I was being irrational and that I was too close to quit now.

"Too close to what? To something I don't want anymore! That's not moving closer. That's moving further away. Oh, and by the way, I'm not quitting. I'm changing directions!"

Then he laughed. *"You're not seriously considering that career in speaking you've been talking about, are you?"*

Those words were my wake-up call. They pierced my heart. I looked at him and said, *"Yes. I don't know how, but that's exactly what I'm going to do. Whatever it takes!"*

I couldn't deny my feelings any longer. I told myself that even though I was confused and scared, I was going to move forward. As soon as I said that, I felt a surge of relief flow through my entire body. I knew that somehow, someway, I would make it work.

That was the first step I took towards embracing this change. The next day I flew back to New York. Within a few weeks, I notified my manager, agent and publicist about my new career move. I thanked them for their years of support, but told them I was no longer in need of their services.

My plan was to do my own bookings to save on commissions, and to continue working the comedy circuit while pursuing a career in speaking. A career, mind you, that I knew absolutely nothing about.

Once I surrendered to these changes, I made a commitment to follow my heart's desire. It was with this commitment that everything started falling into place it was as if the universe and all of its wealth and glory opened itself up to me and said, *"That's it! Now you have got it! You are finally on the right path and here is your reward!"*

Answers to prayers were coming from all directions. It was not uncommon for me to get up and drive to a bookstore to pick out a book or tape at random that would have invaluable information. People I hardly knew helped launch my speaking career. Some I met a workshops and seminars. Others I met through casual conversation on a plane.

You must always make an effort to follow your heart's desire; even if it means changing your entire life. It's the voice of your soul, the radar that guides you to stay centered on love. Allow it to show you the way to the fulfillment of your dreams. It does not have logic, it does not always tell you why, it may cause discomfort and confusion, but it does know exactly what you need to be happy.

When you embrace change and surrender to the beckoning of your heart, it does not mean you are giving up. Rather, it means you are letting go and yielding to something greater. You are letting go and letting God in. I was not quitting stand-up comedy. I was letting go and yielding to a greater purpose—a new dream.

The problem is that sometimes we see the dream, we see the big picture, but we lack the faith and patience that are necessary to make it manifest into our lives.

Without faith and patience, we run the risk of smothering our heart's desire. Whether it's time, hard work, or the changing of old ways and beliefs, there is always something to give up, to let go of or surrender to. This doesn't mean it is a bad thing. In fact, it's a good thing, because our payments, hard times and sacrifices are part of the experience. From the experience comes the nourishment and total expression of our soul.

This could be a major reason why so many people are not enjoying what they have. They may appear to have fulfilled their dreams and goals, but they bypassed certain steps along the way, they took shortcuts to success. As my mysterious angel-friend said, *"Take one step at a time..."* By skipping certain steps they have negated the process, voided the experience, left their souls undernourished.

161

They cheated themselves from enjoying the benefits of what they accomplished. In reality, we have not really accomplished anything if we did not experience the process. It is through experiencing the process that we grow, learn and become. If you do not allow yourself to experience the process, you cannot learn. If you do not learn, you will not grow, if you do not grow, you will not become.

A sense of humor can help guide through the process of following your dreams. Your *humor being* helps you appreciate what you have during the process. And it gives you hope and faith to carry on, regardless of you mistakes and failures.

When you choose to laugh off your disappointments and setbacks that often come with change you build a wall of confidence. You are sending a message to yourself that you are in control of the situation, instead of the situation controlling you. When you let your sense of humor become your sense of perspective, your dreams stay in focus. Your goals remain positive and obtainable. This is true because the fear that represents your mistakes and failures is no longer threatening. You realize your fears and doubts are just a part of the process.

One of the most valuable lessons I've learned from all the changes in my life was that nothing in life is wasted if you learn from it. I now know that every step forward and backward along the way was necessary to prepare me to recognize and receive the gift when it was revealed to me. The seven years of college were not wasted. The years of teaching and counseling were not a mistake. And the eighteen years of comedy were the best years of my life. I needed every experience, the good and the bad, the successes and the failures, the pain and the glory to help me grow. In time, all change comes together full circle. And as the circle continues, I can honestly say I am grateful for all of my feelings and emotions. I am grateful for the peace and anger, and the love and fear.

We must stop looking at the changes in our lives as if they were curses bestowed upon us. Rather, go inside and know that all change is an opportunity to experience, to learn, to grow and to become—and look for the blessing in disguise.

For many people the fear of changing a lifestyle or risking failure is so powerful that they will stay confined in their miserable existence and forever forfeit taking a chance. They concentrate on what is being taken from them, instead of acknowledging the fact that they have a choice on how to deal with it. Along with forfeiting their right to choose, they extinguish all hope and chance of opportunity.

Many of us hold on too tightly to painful jobs, losses, unhappy relationships, and material things. We are not aware that this holding on projects the image of ourselves into the universe. It's no wonder that when these things leave us, our very existence is threatened. They have become a part of who we think we are. If we just let go and relinquish the urge to take control, life will show us the opportunity within the challenge. We will experience the growth of the soul and observe moments of who we really are. When we allow ourselves to embrace the changes that rip us apart and trust that we will be OK, when we let go and follow our hearts rather than our fears, we will live fuller and richer lives as a result.

I believe that whenever a door is slammed shut in our lives, there is an open window with a light shining through. That light is a ray of hope. I call it "Saving Grace." Saving Grace is one of the most powerful miracles you will ever experience. It doesn't necessarily replace what was lost or turn things around to the way they used to be. Rather it replenishes your faith. It comes into your life and lifts you up. It gives you a newfound reason and willpower to live, love, laugh and be happy in spite of the circumstance.

SAVING GRACE

In 1980 I was a counselor at a high school on Long Island. On one particular morning the assistant principal informed me that there was a young girl in his office whose father had passed away. He asked if I would drive her home. Her name was Gina. At 16 she was at the beginning stage of experiencing one of life's most painful lessons, the death of a loved one.

Gina only lived five minutes from the school, but the drive seemed like it was taking forever. I desperately searched to find the right words to ease her pain. What I remember most is the awkward silence and the many tears. I don't know why, but I took her grief more personally then I knew I should. I remember thinking that someone who was so young and innocent should not have to suffer so. When I drove into her driveway I reached over and touched her hand and reminded her that if she wanted someone to talk to, she knew where my office was. She tried to say thank you, but could only nod and get out of the car.

Gina visited my office on many occasions. What eventually developed was more than your everyday student-teacher relationship; it was a heartfelt friendship. Eventually Gina graduated from high school and I left my job as an educator to pursue my career as a stand-up comedian. Through the years Gina would occasionally show up when I performed at a local club. Often we would go out somewhere after the show and talk for hours. It was around this time that I noticed the girl who used to come to my office was now a beautiful, intelligent woman.

It wasn't long before my comedy career took off. In a very short time I was headlining clubs all over the country. Almost two years went by before I saw or heard from Gina. One night she called me when I was performing at a club on Long Island. She told me she was thinking about me, and then asked if I would like to have dinner at her place before I left town again. I accepted the invitation. I continued to see her on a regular basis.

Within a few years, the girl I drove home on a cold February day in 1980 became my wife.

The reason I tell you this story is because Gina and I are both aware that our love for each other is not only her saving grace, but mine as well. We are always there for each other, yet we give ourselves enough space to grow individually. I believe we are soul mates. I always tell her that I loved her long before I ever met her.

There is one common bond that Gina and I share more than anything else. That's our sense of humor. Our *humor beings* have always guided us through the tough times. I find it absolutely amazing the lessons I've learned by observing the way she lives. She has an incredible ability to laugh off her mistakes, misfortunes, and setbacks. She also has an uncanny way of making people not only appreciate but cherish the simple things in life. She truly is the motivation behind the motivator. It's funny how sometimes the teacher becomes the student.

Our relationship continues to blossom and grow. The lessons we learn from each other are priceless. Our relationship was created through the death of her father. That's not to say that she's happy her father passed away. Rather Gina was willing and open to receive the gift of love when it was offered.

Our love for each other is her ray of hope, her open window with the light shining through. She took her first step into the light that very day, years ago, when she chose to accept my invitation to stop by my office to talk. That choice allowed the powers of saving grace to perform miracles in both of our lives.

The reason some people never experience the splendor of saving grace is because they do not allow themselves to see the open window. They are too preoccupied with focusing all of their energy on the door that was closed. They try endlessly, to the point of exhaustion, to pry the door open, so that they can go back to the comfort of the past, to the certainty of the way it used to be. This only intensifies the loss and it leaves them wide open for fear and anger to set in.

The only way to find your open window is to let go of the doorknob, turn around and move on with your life. Let go of your desire to take control. Take every step with faith in yourself and in God. Somewhere along your journey, your window will be there, waiting to guide you and show you a new way. When you find it, walk into the light and embrace a world filled with hope and possibilities.

Often when a traumatic event occurs in our lives, we don't or can't understand the significance. We ask ourselves, *"Why?"*

Let's face it. Sometimes there are not enough reasons

or answers to explain our losses and pain, but God always gives us enough peace to live with it. If we make a conscious choice to challenge our fears, we will find that, with time and understanding, we will view the event from a different, healthier perspective. We will see it was necessary for our spiritual growth. It's this peace and understanding that is also a part of saving grace.

If we let fear of the unknown and uncertainty stop us from taking chances and moving forward we will stifle our true potential. We will remain stagnant in our security and become prisoners of our past. There will be no growth, only empathy and disorder. Deepak Chopra says that without uncertainty and the unknown, life would be boring and meaningless. You will become the victim of the past and live a life of worn-out memories. When you take that leap of faith into the unknown and walk the path of uncertainty, you will walk into the field of opportunity and possibility. You will experience the fun of life, the magic and celebration of your spirit. This is what happens when you embrace change.

Four Ways Humor Helps You Embrace Change

The following four techniques can help you embrace the changes in your life.

1. Acknowledge or admit to yourself that you are getting stressed out or perhaps experiencing some kind of fear or pain about a particular change that is taking place.

It might be the loss of or a change in your job or business. Perhaps it's the death of a loved one or the end of a long relationship. It could be the loss of a home or the uncertainty of moving to a different location. Maybe you were suddenly inflicted with a disease or physically or mentally handicapped because of an accident. Whatever the change is, in order for the healing process to begin it is essential that you acknowledge your pain and fear.

This is where a sense of humor can have a tremendous impact. My friend Steve is a perfect example of how your *humor being* can help you acknowledge your fears. His ability to find the humor in being HIV positive helped him put his fears in perspective. When he allowed himself to laugh in the face of fear, he began to take control. Humor was one of the compelling forces that gave him the courage to embrace the drastic changes that have taken place in his life.

2. Have faith and be willing to move forward in spite of fear and the Destroyers Of The Spirit. This is perhaps the toughest step. The key word is faith. Faith perceives the impossible, it directs you to make a conscious choice to move forward with confidence, that there is light, even when you are surrounded by darkness. A conscious choice to move forward sends a message from the soul to the brain that you are in control of the change, instead of it having control of you.

Faith is not easy to hold onto when the odds are so much against you. Your *humor being* can help you acquire the faith that is needed to embrace change. When humor nourishes the soul, faith is easier to hold onto. My brother Michael was constantly nourishing his soul with laughter. His *humor being* guided him to take steps that the experts said he couldn't. With each step, Michael defied the odds and created miracles in his life. With each miracle, his faith became stronger. Eventually his faith became stronger than his greatest fear.

Prayer, meditation, and quiet time alone (perhaps a walk through nature or writing your feelings in a journal), are also ways to replenish and nurture your faith. Talk to God. Ask for guidance and be alert for a casual reply in the form of a book or a conversation with a friend, in the words of a song or something you hear on television. Recite positive affirmations and visualize how you want your life to be. Believe it is so, make the proper plans, and take action.

3. Nourish your soul with *Love* and *Compassion*. Give. Be kind to yourself and others. These are healing elements that will cast out fear and the Destroyers Of The Spirit. They will help you appreciate what you have, instead of concentrating on what you don't have.

    Sometimes it is helpful to seek counseling or to join a support group. Support groups help you realize that you are not alone. Everyone within the group is experiencing the same kind of fear and pain. They just have different stories to tell. Others also have a way to help you see the humor in your particular situation.

When Naomi Judd was diagnosed with a life-threatening illness, she was forced to leave a lifestyle she had come to know and love. The walls of fear and uncertainty began to close in on her. She made a constant effort to surround herself with love and humor. She shared her pain with loved ones, who in turn helped her nourish her soul with prayer, love, compassion, and of course, their unique brand of humor.

In time, Naomi was able to find her open window with a light shining through. With ongoing courage she embraced the light and walked into the field of possibilities. Her determination and faith enabled her to experience saving grace, which was the discovery of a new self. She now shares her wisdom and inspires people throughout the world.

4. Think positively. The act of positive self-talk will not only strengthen your character, but also your soul. It is beneficial for you to ask yourself what good can come out of even the most challenging situation, no matter how bleak life may seem. It will be difficult, if not impossible, for you to seek opportunity (your open window) if fear, anger, hatred, guilt, blame, self-doubt and resentment overwhelm you.

As you have seen in steps one, two and three, finding the humor in the changes that take place in your life is essential in order to achieve a healthier outcome. Humor extinguishes the wrath of fear. Once the fear has been dissipated, it is important that you feed yourself with positive self-talk.

Instead of asking *"Why me?"* and thinking it is the end of your world as you know it ask yourself empowering questions that will feed your brain to register positive answers and create positive feelings. For example:

What is good about this change that is occurring?

What can I learn from this?

Where can I go for help?

What needs to be done for me to overcome my anger and fear?

This is an opportunity for me to grow emotionally and spiritually.

In time this will pass and I will be stronger.

These types of questions and statements let you see the advantages in your challenge, instead of only the disadvantages. It's not the changes that take place in your life that cause you to panic or to be consumed by fear. Instead it's how you perceive change that makes the difference. If what you think becomes your reality, then you should create a thinking system that will lead you to take actions that will be advantageous, in spite of the situation.

Your perception of yourself and the world around you determines the quality of happiness you will have. If you think you are weak, inadequate, or victimized then the energy you send out will mirror those thoughts. It will be difficult, if not impossible, to feel happy when harboring such thoughts.

If you believe you are powerful and view life as a never-ending learning experience filled with choices, and if you choose to allow your *humor being* the freedom to laugh off hard times and your deepest fears, you will formulate within yourself a sense of hope. Then the energy you send out will mirror those thoughts, enabling you to lead a more fulfilling and happier life.

HIGH POINTS TO REMEMBER

❧ When you embrace change you are surrendering to a certain trust; an unshakable faith that somehow, someway, some good will result from even the most tragic situation.

❧ If you let fear of the unknown stop you from taking chances, you will stifle your true potential.

❧ The four ways humor helps you accept change are extremely beneficial in helping you embrace any change that takes place in your life.

Bibliography

Buscaglia, Leo, Ph.D. *Living, Loving & Learning*. Ballantine Books, 1983.

Butterworth, Eric. *Discover The Power Within You*. Harper & Row Publishers.

Carlson, Richard, Ph.D. *You Can Be Happy No Matter What*. New World Library, 1992.

Chopra, Deepak. *The Seven Spiritual Laws of Success*. Amber-Allen Publishing, 1994.

Csikszentmihalyi, Mihaly. *Flow*. Simon & Schuster, 1994.

Dyer, Wayne W. *Manifest Your Destiny*. Harper Collins, 1997.

Frankl, Viktor E. *Man's Search For Meaning*. Washington Square Press, 1984.

Goleman, Daniel. *Emotional Intelligence*. Bantam Press, 1995.

Judd, Naomi. *Love Can Build A Bridge*. Ballantine Books, 1993.

Mandino, Og. *The Choice*. Bantam Press, 1984.

Peck, M. Scott, M.D. *The Road Less Traveled*. Simon & Schuster, 1978.

Sinetar, Marsha. *Do What You Love, The Money Will Follow*. Dell Publishing, 1987.

Williamson, Marianne. *A Return To Love*. Harper Collins, 1992.

Order Information

To order *Becoming A Humor Being* and other products by
Steve Rizzo:

Telephone: **1-866-292-7911**
or E-mail: **mail@steverizzo.com**

For information on Steve Rizzo's keynote presentations
and seminars, please contact Laugh It Off Productions:

Telephone: **847-832-9775**
or E-mail: **michele@steverizzo.com**
Website: **www.steverizzo.com**